Detail from Second Edition Ordnance Survey Map of 1895.

OLD MITCHAM

Tom Francis

OLD MITCHAM

Tom Francis

Edited by

Eric Montague

With best wishes

Eric Montague

6-11-'93.

Phillimore

1993

Published by
PHILLIMORE & CO. LTD.
Shopwyke Manor Barn, Chichester, Sussex

ISBN 0 85033 862 X

Printed and bound in Great Britain by
BIDDLES LTD.
Guildford, Surrey

This book is dedicated to Tom Francis in gratitude for his foresight in recording his reminiscences of an Old Mitcham that has now passed beyond living memory.

List of Illustrations

Frontispiece: Tom Francis

Acknowledgements

Thanks are due to Paul Harper, Chairman of the Leisure Services Committee of the London Borough of Merton, for considering and agreeing to publication of this book; to Michael Saich, until retirement in 1992 the Borough Librarian, for lending his invaluable support to the undertaking; and to Penny Parker, Acting Borough Librarian, Susan Andrew, Reference Librarian at Mitcham Library, and Keith Skone, Local Studies Librarian, without whose help it would never have been accomplished.

Foreword

It was on the evening of 22 February 1943 that Tom Francis, then in his early 70s, embarked on the self-imposed task of recording 'what I know about Mitcham, where I have lived all my life so far: and recording too the stories and information I received from my father, who was also native born'. Both, in fact, had been born within sight of the Cricket Green and from their earliest years had been 'familiar with the crack of bat and ball and the sight of cricket on the green'.

When a young man, Tom Francis had assembled an impressive collection of some 300 lantern slides of Mitcham, a number of which dated to the 1860s, and 50 years later he was still showing them to appreciative audiences. Taking advantage of the lull in the bombing by the German Luftwaffe, which during the Blitz of 1940-41 took such a toll of lives and property in Mitcham, Tom Francis had recently catalogued and indexed this collection. He shared with many of his contemporaries the feeling that 'Mitcham's story should be recorded', and it was for this reason, and for the sake of his slides, which he realised needed something more than captions if their full value was not to be lost to future generations, that he set to work. As if sensing that he might be interrupted – he was to be injured himself during a renewal of the bombing, which resulted in the loss of an eye – he commented at the outset that writing would be 'at odd times, and as memory serves'. In the event, the notes were not completed until after the war, some of the latest entries being dated to 1947.

Following his death in August 1953 at the age of 81, the Tom Francis Collection of Slides, together with his 'Lecture Notes', was presented by his daughter to the Borough of Mitcham with the expressed wish that they should form the basis of an annual Tom Francis Lecture. That wish has been honoured faithfully by the Library Service for 40 years, and the audiences which have packed the lecture room on each occasion have borne witness not only to the enduring fascination of Tom Francis's slides, but also to the success of his efforts at telling what he knew of the history of his beloved Mitcham.

Although familiar to those few who have been privileged to be invited to deliver the annual lecture, Tom Francis's notes have never been published, and have therefore not been available to wider readership. In recent years a few of the photographs have been reproduced in calendars and other publications of the London Borough of Merton, but to a large extent this rich legacy also has remained out of reach of the general public. To enable this situation to be rectified, as well as for security purposes, in 1992 the Borough's Education and Recreation Department had photographic prints made from all the surviving negatives. This has greatly facilitated the publication of a selection from the slide collection, which forms the basis of this book.

Choice of the illustrations used in 'Old Mitcham' has, of necessity, been restricted by the need to keep within the publisher's guidelines, whilst at the same time ensuring reasonable coverage of the range of subjects portrayed by Tom Francis. A few have been omitted since they have been reproduced already, notably in *Mitcham: A Historical Glimpse*, published by Merton Library Service, or in my own *Mitcham: A Pictorial History*. With two exceptions I have resisted the temptation to include other contemporary photographs of Mitcham not actually part of the Tom Francis slide collection since I feel this work should, essentially, be a tribute to his contribution to the compilation of a history of the emerging township. The two photographs which are departures from this principle are of the Manor House, and the first 100 members of the Berkeley Teetotal Society. Both are included in the section devoted to the Pitt family, who exerted such an influence in Tom's formative years.

Tom Francis appreciated at the outset that his notes would be disjointed, and they clearly were not intended for publication in the form in which they were presented to the Borough Librarian. As a consequence, some editing of the supportive material has been unavoidable but, again, this has been kept to a minimum and as far as possible Tom Francis's original comments have been retained. The urge to add to the basic text has also been resisted, except where Tom's comments seem to need a little amplification for the benefit of present day readers.

Given the prominence of the fair and village cricket in the annual calendar of events in late Victorian Mitcham, it was inevitable that these should have loomed large in Tom Francis's memories. Both have received excellent treatment in two recent publications – *Mitcham Fair* published by Merton Library Services (which drew on Tom Francis's notes to a considerable extent), and the souvenir brochure *300 Years of Mitcham Cricket* written by Tom Higgs for Mitcham Cricket Club and published in 1985. For this reason it was felt it would be acceptable for both subjects to be afforded somewhat less space in this book than would otherwise have been the case, whilst at the same time not losing sight of the importance rightly given to them by Tom Francis as cornerstones of his history of Old Mitcham.

ERIC MONTAGUE

Sutton, March 1993

The Slides, the Cameras and the Photographers

In the main, the collection of slides Tom Francis had assembled was from negatives of his own taking, and dated from the early 1890s. A few later slides had been given to him by friends, but two groups were somewhat earlier in date. The larger of these comprised slides made from wet-plate negatives produced between 1865 and 1870 by a professional photographer named Drummond, employed by Thomas Francis senior. Drummond was at the time actively recording scenes in Wallington, Carshalton and Beddington as well as Mitcham (Pl.1). These, we are told by Tom Francis, were published in the old 'carte-de-visite' size, mounted and sold at 6d. each. Elsewhere in his notes Tom recalls a collection of '50 beautiful photographic views of Mitcham', taken for George Pitt and sold in 1870 at 6d. each or 4s.6d. a dozen by Tom's father at the London House stores. Although he does not make it clear, it seems likely that it was actually from the negatives of these views that the slides acquired by Tom were produced. The other early component of the collection, numbering a dozen or so slides, can be attributed to John Robert Chart who, like Tom Francis, had an abiding love for old Mitcham and dabbled a little in photography in the early wet-plate days. Chart's slides, although in Tom's opinion technically not of the highest quality, provide rare glimpses of the village in the 1870s and '80s. The coverage of the collection as a whole is, therefore, of considerable historic interest.

Tom Francis believed his father did a little printing and mounting, but never heard from him that he had ever actually used a camera. The cupboard of a little mahogany sideboard in the family home was used as Thomas Francis senior's chemical and paper store, and the mysterious bottles and a few pieces of apparatus aroused young Tom's early interest, but, as he said, in the 1880s the 'amateur had little encouragement from the manufacturers to spend his money'.

The camera Tom used in his own first youthful foray into commercial photography was of the mahogany box type with a rack-work lens – the type then commonly employed by professionals at seaside holiday resorts – utilising the convenient dry-plate which had become available. His friend John Marsh Pitt was his partner in the enterprise, and although now and then they produced some fair results, on the whole, Tom admits, they had little to boast about. They were, nevertheless, optimists and bought a rubber stamp bearing the name of their firm – 'Pitt and Francis, Photo', and if not able to make money hoped at best to pay for their experimenting. Their charge of 6d. a copy to their friendly clients, with a slight reduction per half dozen, was not considered excessive, but even then bad stock accumulated, and the two boys were glad to offer clearing lines at 3s.6d. for a dozen assorted photographs. Later, Tom Francis was to purchase what he called 'a Guinea Griffiths hand camera'. Only one example of these early ventures survived as a slide when he came to catalogue his collection 50 years later (Pl.4).

On coming of age in 1893 Tom Francis received from fellow members of the Berkeley Mutual Improvement Society, of which John's father was a leading light, the handsome present of 'a really first-class camera by Marion of Soho', which he describes as having a 'Half plate R/R lens rising front, [and] 3 double dark slides with wooden tripod'. The first exposure – of Whitford Lane, looking south – was certainly a success, and is the second in the selection of his slides reproduced in this book (Pl.2).

Further successes fuelled his enthusiasm, and many of the more interesting photographs in Tom Francis's collection date from 1893. In the years to come he was to possess both quarter-plate and full-plate cameras, which he used in a semi-professional way for groups, especially at weddings. A 'Memo Freud' camera holding 40 flat notched films 'like a pack of cards' was a special favourite until the handy folding spool cameras came on the market, and a birthday gift from his wife of 'a folding Soho with Beck lens and ducal finder' was to prove a great companion and gave 'no end of pleasure to others besides myself'.

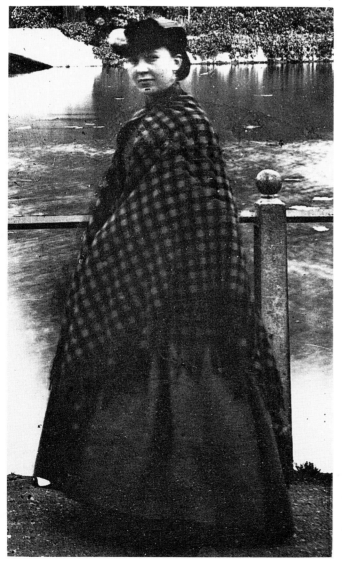

1. A young woman in a crinoline and a 'pork pie' hat. Although out of fashion by the time Tom Francis was a small boy, he could just remember the style lingering on into the late 1870s. In the background to this photograph, which Tom dated to 1868, one can just discern the Leoni bridge at The Grove, Carshalton, suggesting that it must be an example of Drummond's work.

2. Whitford Lane, in 1893, looking south. This was one of the first photographs taken by Tom Francis with the half-plate camera he received as a gift on his twenty-first birthday. A few historical comments are warranted, drawing on Tom's own notes. On the left, following sale of the Elmwood estate in 1905, a row of shops were to be built. These included a motor-garage and Mitcham's general post office and telephone exchange built in the 1930s. Hodges' estate office is just visible in the distance on the left. To the right are gateposts and front garden walls of Glebe Villas, four pairs of semi-detached late-Victorian villas occupied by what Tom Francis referred to as 'better middle-class Mitchamers'. During the 1920s and '30s most of these villas were converted into flats. On 22 June 1944 a 'Doodle Bug', or 'VI', fell on Thrushcroft, one of a pair of substantial houses built by Athol Harwood on a field left between Glebe Villas, opposite the post office. Thrushcroft and its neighbour Athelstan were both destroyed, as were several of the Glebe Villas. The rest, plus Hodges' office and the Lodge further down towards the Cricket Green, were severely damaged. By December 1945 the site of the villas had been cleared and was occupied by Nissen huts, erected as temporary housing by Italian prisoners-of-war. Athol Harwood, who died at Thrushcroft in 1944, was the son-in-law of James Southerton, the Surrey and Mitcham cricketer. He is remembered for having left £100 to Mitcham Cricket Club, to be invested to provide a presentation bat for the most promising young cricketer during the season. A keen gardener all his life – the garden of Thrushcroft had been his pride – Harwood also left a bequest of £100 to Mitcham Horticultural Society.

3. A few of the slides shown by Tom Francis were from photographs taken by Charles Matthews, who had a hairdresser's and confectioner's shop overlooking the Cricket Green, close to the *White Hart*. Charles possessed a stereoscopic camera, with which he produced a series of views of Mitcham. Here he is seen recording groups at Mitcham Fair, probably within a year or so of the accession of Edward VII.

The Francis Family

4. The only slide surviving from Tom Francis's early ventures into photography in the early 1890s is this portrait of his parents, Thomas and Eliza, posing in the garden at the back of their shop, London House, in Whitford Lane. Thomas Francis senior has his eyes fixed in what his son described as 'a celestial gaze'.

5. Tom Francis, striking a cricketing pose, photographed here in the early 1890s, probably in the back garden of London House. He was a cricketing enthusiast and a loyal supporter of Mitcham village cricket throughout his long life. In his younger days Tom played regularly in the Upper Mitcham v. Lower Mitcham cricket matches, and when the Wednesday XI was revived in 1925 there were few matches he missed.

6. In general, he tells us, Tom Francis's family were patient sitters, and it is therefore to be expected that several of them should feature in his slide collection. His father, in the garden where in later years he spent much of his time, appears in two of them.

7. One of Tom Francis's favourite photos of his father shows him nursing a huge marrow weighing over 56lbs. which he grew in his kitchen garden during the First World War.

8. Children are irresistible subjects for proud parents with a camera, and one summer's day in 1910 a mischievous Kathleen and John Francis playing in the garden with a large rhubarb leaf were 'captured' by their father in this delightful study.

The Charts

John R. (the 'R' – for Robert – was usually used to distinguish him from his father, John Chart) and Mary Chart were remembered by Tom Francis with affection as gentle, unassuming people who, having no family of their own, acted as foster or godparents to hundreds of Mitcham youngsters (Pl.9). Besides being a corn and seed merchant John was also a funeral undertaker, a trade followed by his father before him. John was ever loyal to the memory of his parents, and when he was within easy reach of three score years and ten his trade advertisements announced that 'he still carried on the business of his late father'. Mary conducted a Bible class for young women, and John was a preacher of local repute, who led a mission for adults in his workshop in Clarendon Grove, and 'did not stand on ceremony'. But the Charts were best known for running a Band of Hope for the young people of Mitcham. For how many years Tom did not know,

> but generation after generation passed through the Band of Hope and John and Mary's influence went with them, or some of them, to the 'uttermost parts of the earth'. By concerts during the winter money was raised to take the children to Brighton free of charge every year. Parents and friends could buy tickets for 2s.6d. and Chart's excursion to Brighton became a red letter day for Mitcham. The tickets for the Band of Hope concerts were printed by John himself; they were not good examples of the printer's art, but made it known that admission to the concert could be gained by the payment of 2d. Reserved seats, however, were 4d.

John Chart was a pioneer photographer of the 'wet-plate' days, and gave young Tom Francis some useful tips on the art. John did a bit of photography professionally, and he was also Mitcham's lanternist, making his own oxygen for his 'limelight'. 'Old Mitcham' was his favourite subject and, as we have seen, a number of his slides found their way into Tom's collection.

John Chart's popularity and kindliness ensured him a place at the top of the poll in early parish council elections, and in 1904 he was elected Chairman. As might have been expected, he was regarded as something of a specialist in regulations concerning burials.

9. A flashlight photograph of John R. and Mary (Polly) Chart in their sitting room behind the corn and seed shop at the corner of Fair Green near the *Three Kings* pond. Tom Francis recalled the Charts' sitting room as 'quite extraordinary'. The mirror on the mantleshelf was surrounded by scores of letters with documents tucked behind it. The piano (or was it an organ?) could not be seen for piles of magazines and newspapers, years out of date, stacked on the keyboard and heaped on top. The couch was also piled high with its collection of papers, and for the visitor to sit down a few square inches had to be cleared. It was here that Tom first thrilled to the sound of the new phonograph, with its cylindrical records, and received useful tips from John on the art of photography.

10. John Chart's undertaker's workshop in Clarendon Grove doubled as a mission room, his bench, tools and sometimes coffins being screened by curtains when the mission was in session. Here the Charts' Band of Hope met and the adult Bible class, conducted by John. The room was also used for the evening entertainments organised by the Charts to help raise funds for the annual Brighton excursion. On such occasions it was customary for proceedings to commence with the appointment of a chairman, sometimes the vicar. Turns consisted of songs, recitations, dialogues, sketches and musical items given mostly by youthful members of the Band of Hope, but augmented by contributions from John and Mary Chart, helpers (who were not necessarily total abstainers) and friends. 'Admission tickets', recalled Tom Francis, 'usually bore the information, very seldom needed by the audience, "Carriages at 9.30". However, whatever the quality of the performance, everyone seemed to enjoy the shows, and listened with marked respect to the wise words of the Chairman. The special performances were held in St. Mark's Parish Room, and occasionally in the Vestry Hall, with Magic Lantern, Phonograph, or the Mitcham Brass Band.'

11. The Charts' annual excursion to Brighton (known as 'Chartses') was the great event in Old Mitcham round about 1890-91. Schools closed and trade was slack – in fact Mitcham seemed empty. People might be seen making their way to Mitcham Junction station an hour or more before the Brighton train (an excursion special) was due to start. John Chart with his 'staff' and chief supporters went down in style by Pullman. It was an honour to share this luxury! Headed by George the porter, the railway staff seemed to be infected with the general excitement, and George's great voice, which could be heard easily down the line at Beddington Halt, boomed instructions to everyone.

12. Once at Brighton many of the children experienced for the first time in their lives the fun of playing in the sea. Two or three packed into a bathing machine and then walked gingerly over the pebbles to the water's edge. Costumes were very ill-fitting and, whereas those worn by the men and boys might be scant, the girls' were well on the way to their ankles. Old bathing women in dark serge garments looked after the safety and welfare of the smaller children. Swimmers were few, but adventurous souls, braving the waves, clung to the safety rope with much shrieking, and bobbed up and down, to the amusement of the onlookers. If courage failed for a real dip – it was, after all, only once a year – there was always the lesser joy of paddling. 'So, here we are in the picture,' Tom Francis used to say to audiences at his lantern slide lectures many years later, 'Good plain honest calico in 1890 – no fancy colours – no artificial silk! – no rayon!' Finally came the journey home, the children tired and pink from too much sun, but clutching their trophies of seaweed, shells, crabs and Brighton rock and, of course, presents from the seaside for those unfortunates at home who had missed the fun. 'Ah well,' said Tom, 'thems were the days!'

The Pitt Family

Like the Francis family, the Pitts were members of the Society of Friends, and their son John Marsh Pitt became a life-long friend of Tom Francis. The Pitts feature in several of the older slides in Tom's collection, and his accompanying notes throw an intriguing light on the activities of what was a most unusual, if not eccentric, family.

George Pitt senior, John Marsh's grandfather, was the founder and proprietor of the drapery store in Whitford Lane which was eventually to become the property of Thomas Francis's father. The story began c.1830, when one of a pair of semi-detached 18th-century houses immediately to the south of Mitcham's Fair Green was offered for sale. Pitt, who had retired from his drapery business in Camden Town, was returning through Mitcham from Brighton by stagecoach when he noticed the 'For Sale' board. Alighting from the coach, he inspected the property and decided to purchase. Amongst the effects he removed from north London were some of his best drapery stock, which he exhibited on the front railings of his new house. Such was the interest shown by Mitcham people, that he decided to set up shop again. Edwin Chart, a surveyor and son of John Chart, a local building contractor, was called in, and a shop front – with small panes of glass as was then the fashion – was soon installed and London House had come into being (Pl.13).

London House (the name seems to have been George Pitt senior's inspiration) was originally the southernmost of the two semi-detached three-storeyed houses, each of which had commodious cellars. Steps led up to the front doors, and there were lofts under the red-tiled roofs. There were also side doors, whilst to the rear of the house bought by Pitt was a cobbled yard with a stable and coach house, over which there was a further loft. The garden, understood by Tom Francis to have been a later acquisition, was narrow but over 300 ft. long. To the left was a meadow of the same length, part of the former parish glebe and by Tom's time the property of the Church Commissioners.

At the time Pitt's business was established the only other buildings in Whitford Lane were two weatherboarded cottages, to be seen in several of the photographs of London House, and Elm Lodge at the corner of the Cricket Green. London House in fact was to remain the only shop in Whitford Lane for many years. For a time the right-hand building of the pair became a baker's shop and later still a printer's, visible in a photograph of 1868 (Pl.14). In 1879 both were combined to form a much enlarged London House general stores. No further commercial development occurred in Whitford Lane until after 1900.

Next in this group of photographs is one of George Pitt junior, father of John Marsh Pitt (Pl.15). Shortly after his birth at London House, George's parents appear to have moved away from Mitcham, and for a few years the shop was occupied by an ironmonger. The family returned, however, and George was soon able to assist his father in the drapery business, ownership of which was ultimately to pass to him. George Pitt junior married whilst at London House, but three of his children died within a short period of each other, a tragic sequence of events which may have induced George and his wife to move to Berkeley Cottage, Lower Mitcham in 1869 (Pl.16). London House was left in the care of two trusted assistants, Thomas Francis and Eliza Cooper, who were soon to marry, and the following year they took over the business. In 1886 their son Tom was given a job in the shop, where he was still working in 1944.

George Pitt junior had married Priscilla, daughter of John Finch Marsh and his wife Hannah of Park Lane Croydon, both prominent members of the Society of Friends. Shortly after the birth at Berkeley Cottage of his son, John Marsh Pitt, George conceived the idea of inviting his mother and mother-in-law, both recently widowed, to join his household. Requiring more space he moved from Berkeley Cottage to the Manor House next door, where the two elderly ladies were able to have their separate apartments (Pl.17). In due course little Tom Francis was appointed playmate to Johnnie (there was only seven months' difference in their ages), and the two small boys received daily lessons from Priscilla.

Berkeley Cottage can be seen as the taller of a pair of houses in a photograph of *c.*1870 (Pl.16). The property adjoining was Berkeley House, then occupied by Walter Fry, grandson of the famous Quaker prison reformer and philanthropist Elizabeth Fry. Behind the pair of large wooden gates to the right was Berkeley Place. Here, either side of a central court, a number of very small single storey cottages were let at 3s.6d. to 4s.6d. per week. The site was redeveloped in the 1930s, and is now occupied by a terrace of shops with lock-up garages at the rear accessed from Baron Grove.

George Pitt was regarded by Tom Francis, and no doubt many of his contemporaries, as 'a bit of a character'. A militant local politician, describing himself as a 'Liberal Star in a very dark place', he travelled extensively with his wife, visiting America, Europe and the Near East, including Palestine and Persia, and finally encompassed the globe. On returning to Mitcham, George published an account of their Remarkable Travels in a book which achieved a large sale locally. 'If for no other reason' observed Tom Francis, 'these travels were remarkable for the distance covered at an insignificant cost.'

Local records are a rich source of stories of George Pitt's escapades, but Tom Francis confined his lecture notes to recounting one rather bizarre episode when George, who kept a horse called Jack, insisted on leading the animal around the Manor House kitchen. The reason for the hospitality afforded to Jack is not explained, but fortunately the kitchen was a large one, and we are assured that the animal was well-behaved. In wintry weather, when there was sufficient depth of snow, the old horse 'to his astonishment' was harnessed to a cumbersome wooden sledge, which in Tom's opinion resembled the framework of an ancient four-post bedstead.

At one time two horses were kept in the stables, the animals being required to draw the Pitts' several conveyances, which included a wagonette (preferred for use in bad weather as it could be covered), a dogcart and a brougham. Occasionally these were used to carry Mitcham Friends to the Croydon meetings, with Joseph Rose ('Nimshi junior'), who lived in one of the cottages in Berkeley Place, acting as the family's coachman. The two small boys were often taken for outings in the brougham or wagonette, surviving (and thereafter frequently recounting) such small adventures as being stuck in a pond in Morden Road, and driving through water a foot or so deep at Hackbridge.

13. The London House stores in Whitford Lane. An artist's impression of the shop in the mid-19th century.

Priscilla also drove the wagonette, to the smiles of beholders and rude calls from the village boys, for she dressed in the old Quaker style, complete with 'coal scuttle' bonnet. A Friends' Meeting was held every Sunday morning in the large drawing room of the Manor House, and an additional 'reading' meeting was usually held on Sunday evenings. It was not uncommon for the Pitts to have visiting Friends from Ireland and America staying with them. Figures in Quaker garb were often to be seen at this time in Mitcham even, according to Tom Francis, sliding (and falling) on the Cranmer pond one particularly hard winter. When death finally reduced the size of the Manor House family, the Pitts moved to Berkeley House. Here the meetings continued to be held until the growing families of the members necessitated moving the meeting to a hall which had been built in the garden to house the Berkeley Mutual Improvement Society, another of George Pitt's ventures. When George himself passed on, this Meeting House was re-erected in Berkeley Place.

Priscilla was a staunch teetotaller, and held temperance meetings at the Manor House. A Band of Hope was also organised whilst the family was still living there. Johnnie and Tom, aged eight, were star performers with their recitations of *We're little temperance soldiers* and *Come take a glass of wine with me, No! No! No!* etc. It was later, when John was in his early twenties, that the Berkeley Teetotal Society was started. George, however, did not practise total abstinence, and was allowed to keep a little barrel down in the cellar. In his younger days he had been persuaded to speak in the temperance cause in Mitcham, and as a result of an argument he declared to his wife and son that if they could find 99 staunch teetotallers who would join a society, he would make the hundredth. This seems to have been accomplished without difficulty, and at a special meeting George appeared in sack cloth, and signed. As a final gesture he emptied the barrel containing his rather thin beer down the drain (Pl.18).

The Berkeley Teetotal Society attracted many members through its imaginative calendar of social events, and was soon flourishing. First class speakers came to the monthly meetings in the Vestry Hall, which was usually packed. A fine projecting lantern was bought capable of throwing a 15 ft. picture – with dissolving effects – onto a sheet hanging from the Vestry Hall beams. Competitions and exhibitions of handicrafts were arranged and prizes were offered for collecting 'pledges'; all proved highly popular with an unsophisticated public. One outstanding event recalled by Tom Francis was the presentation of a play entitled *The Trial of John Barleycorn.* The hall was full to overflowing, and a hundred would-be members of the audience had to be turned away. George Pitt took the part of the judge, and John Marsh Pitt counsel for the prosecution, whilst Tom Francis appeared for the defence assisted by his brother, Will, who acted as solicitor. The rest of the cast was played by members of the society, and the show was voted a great success.

When John Marsh Pitt came of age in 1892 a carnival was held in celebration, and Mitcham people enjoyed a week of merriment and competitions arranged at his father's expense (Pl.19). The same year John married Emily H. D. Bell at Waterford, and returned to Mitcham to make a home at Shamrock Villa (Pl.20).

As the Charts had demonstrated, group excursions to the sea were a treat much appreciated by those whose normal lives seldom took them far from the village. On one memorable occasion George Pitt hired two special trains to convey a large number of Berkeley Teetotal Society members on an outing to Brighton, free of charge and, furthermore, provided everyone with cake. Tom Francis and his friend James Drewett elected to cycle to the coast, and were at Brighton station in time to see the arrival of the throng from Mitcham. George Pitt, with Priscilla (in a white shawl) and John Pitt, can just be identified in the centre of the happy crowd, photographed by Tom Francis from the parade (Pl.21).

Other trips followed, including excursions to Portsmouth and an outing to Windsor by horse-drawn brakes, but after some years George Pitt withdrew his interest and, sad to say, the Society gradually faded away.

14. The London House stores in 1868. The building is a typical structure of the mid-18th century. It had probably been erected by Samuel Oxtoby, a local builder, who then owned the land.

15. George Pitt junior, a redoubtable Quaker, who inherited the London House stores from his father. Having no interest in money, he made over the business to his two shop assistants, Thomas Francis and Eliza Cooper.

16. Berkeley Cottage, Lower Mitcham, the home of George and Priscilla Pitt after they left London House. Berkeley Cottage stood next to the Manor House in London Road, between the Cricket Green and today's Baron Grove. Berkeley House is to the right in the photograph and, behind the gates, is Berkeley Place.

17. The Manor House, Lower Mitcham. This large rambling 18th-century house would have been occupied by the Pitts on a lease from William Simpson III who, on the death of his father in 1888, had become lord of the manor of Mitcham and the owner of several of the larger houses in the village.

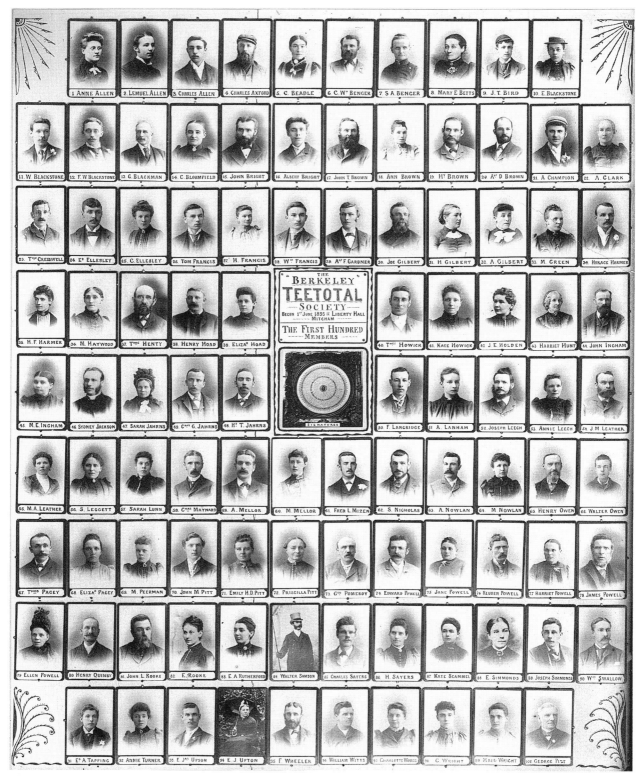

18.   The first 100 members of the Berkeley Teetotal Society. George Pitt (bottom right) became the hundredth member.

19. John Marsh Pitt, Tom Francis's boyhood companion.

20. Emily Pitt, née Bell, wife of John Marsh Pitt. The young couple married in 1892 in Ireland, and on arrival in Mitcham set up home at the appropriately named Shamrock Villa.

21. The Berkeley Teetotal Society on an outing to Brighton.

22. On their first excursion to the sea the Berkeley Teetotal Society had been accompanied by its embryonic brass band, which formed up outside Brighton station on arrival, and led the visitors to the seafront. Tom Francis considered them a rather 'ragtag' lot, although enthusiastic, but a few years later, through the generosity of Mr. Ely of Wimbledon, they were at least to acquire a 'uniform' of bandsmen's hats. As the years passed fewer recruits to the band were strict teetotallers, and with its gradually changing membership the band became first the Gas Works Band, and later the Mitcham Military Brass Band, competent (and confident) enough to take part in a Crystal Palace Brass Band Festival.

Schools and Scholars

Responsibility for the National Schools on Lower Green, opened in 1812 in the enlarged Sunday School building of 1788, was transferred from the church to the newly created local School Board in 1871. Lighting and heating in the old building were grossly inadequate, and ventilation and drainage were also poor, leading to its frequent condemnation by school inspectors. It was not until 1897 when a new school was opened by the Board in Church Road that the old building ceased to be used as a day school. It became known as the 'parish rooms', and at the outbreak of war in 1939 was pressed into service as the local Food Office.

Many noted Mitcham men, like Tom Francis senior, received their primary education at the National Schools for a few pence a week. The subjects taught may have been few, and the standards basic, but the old man often criticised his sons for costing him so much for the results they obtained at more prestigious establishments. One of a series of cartoons drawn by Collingsby, a local resident, and later made into slides by Tom Francis, shows Thomas Compton teaching the boys at the National School in 1878 (Pl.23).

Mitcham Lodge College in the High Street, Upper Mitcham, catered for boys from a different social background. It was located in a former private house (Pl.24), and stood to the south of today's London Road school. After the house had been demolished the land was occupied by a Walls ice cream depot in the 1930s, later becoming a caravan yard. In Tom Francis's youth Dr. William Smith was the college principal. There were several boarders, who were smartly turned out on Sundays with mortar boards and Eton coats and collars, but the scholars were mostly day pupils. The actual schoolroom was in a building at the rear. Tom Francis was at the school for a few months, as was his brother William. Schoolfellows he remembered were Robert and Oswald Green, Charles and Harry Hannington, Charles Lack-Russell from the railway station and Moyse of London Road, Morden. According to Dr. Smith's advertisements, he aimed to prepare his students for a commercial career, but he made no great success of the undertaking. Tom Francis was usually given to understand that he had been sent to the school to offset a small debt owing to his father. There were two Frenchmen in residence learning English, who also taught some French. Their recreation, Tom recalled, was spearing rats with a sword stick in the outhouses. Smith was keen that the boys should know their tables, and every morning the whole school stood and went through every table in the book, or so it seemed to young Tom. Whatever else he absorbed, he used to say, he would always remember that three barleycorns made one inch!

An altogether different type of establishment was the Holborn Industrial Schools in London Road, Upper Mitcham, erected in 1855 as the St George the Martyr (Southwark) Industrial Schools to provide for pauper and orphaned children from the London parish of St George. The schools were transferred to the Board of Guardians of the Holborn Union in 1870 (Pl.27). The facilities were extremely good, and the schools had a small swimming bath, and playing fields which extended back to what is now Bond Road. An infirmary was built in 1882, and a new school, still used by the Education Department of the London Borough of Merton, in 1892.

The Holborn Schools had accommodation for 400 boys, girls and infants, cared for by a staff of 80 under a superintendent matron. The older children were smartly dressed in uniforms, the girls in cloaks and the boys in corduroys and peaked caps. They were a familiar sight in Mitcham, the teachers ushering their charges along the streets in long 'crocodiles' when they were taken out for walks, or were attending services at the parish church. The Holborn Schools Band was much in request at village celebrations and school treats. In later years Tom Francis used to recall the enduring vision of the self-important little bandmaster, dressed in top hat and frock coat, proudly leading his boys. Some were very small, and carried instruments quite out of proportion to their size, but they succeeded in producing sounds of amazing volume.

Through much of the 18th and 19th centuries large houses in Mitcham were used, for varying periods, as private boarding academies for the sons and daughters of upper class families or of members of the armed forces and colonial service stationed abroad. By Tom Francis's day the phenomenon was passing, and a large weatherboarded house in Upper Mitcham, facing Figges Marsh, was one of the last (Pl.28). Known as The Poplars Academy, it was used as a boarding and day school for young gentlemen throughout much of the Victorian period, and a number of boys from the more wealthy families in Mitcham received their education here. According to Tom Francis the building was demolished, probably in the mid-1880s, after there had been an outbreak of scarlet fever at the school. The academy is now commemorated in the name of Poplar Avenue, the houses of which occupy much of the site of the building and its grounds.

23. Thomas Compton, impressively bearded, imparting pearls of wisdom to boys at the National School, Lower Green, in 1878. From the careful drawing of the assistant teacher and the boys in the front row one may assume they were intended to be good likenesses. Compton himself was a keen cricketer.

MASTER. "Now boys! I want to give you a word of advice. Never be Conceited. You may be able to play at Cricket, you may be good at Skating, proficient in Arithmetic and many other accomplishments, but never allow these small things to make you Conceited. If you do, take my word for it you will be certain 'get yourselves disliked'"

24. A group of girls from the British Schools in Merton Lane (now Western Road), photographed on May Day, *c.*1890. The school had been founded in 1857 under the auspices of the British and Foreign Schools Society and used premises owned by the Congregational church. According to Tom Francis the boys' department had been closed down when Killick's Lane (later St Mark's Road) school was built by the Local School Board in 1884.

25. Mitcham Lodge College, Upper Mitcham. The site, just to the south of Eagle House, now lies mainly beneath the new road by-passing the Upper Green.

26. Dr. Smith and scholars in the grounds of Mitcham Lodge College on a parents' open day. The rear of Mitcham Lodge, unlike the front, was timber-framed and weatherboarded, as was the single-storey school room, just visible behind the doctor.

27. The impressive building of the Holborn Industrial Schools in London Road, Upper Mitcham. The pond in the foreground was one of many surviving in Mitcham in the closing years of the last century, and belonged to Pound Farm. It was filled in by Mizen Brothers, the market gardeners, and greenhouses were erected on the spot before the end of the century.

28. The Poplars Boarding Academy for Young Gentlemen, run by Albert Grover until the mid-1880s, after which it was closed down.

Church and Chapel

Tom Francis used to begin talks on the parish church of St Peter and St Paul at Mitcham with a slide showing an engraving of the old medieval church which had been published in 1800 (Pl.29). This stone and flint building dated to the 13th century and had been extended and repaired repeatedly over the years. The most noteworthy repairs took place between 1638-40 after the church was struck by lightning and was partially destroyed by fire during a storm which severely damaged 13 other churches in Surrey. When the old church was being demolished in 1819 prior to rebuilding, the lower part of the medieval tower was found to be sound enough to warrant retention, and was incorporated in the present church.

The new church was consecrated in 1822. Its external appearance was to be altered somewhat before the end of the century, but in one of the earliest slides in the Tom Francis collection, dating to about 1865, the church can be seen very much as it appeared when newly completed (Pl.30). A major feature, soon to be removed during the formation of a baptistry, was the original entrance to the church, beneath the great west window. The new building was not well received by connoisseurs of the true gothic style, and one guide book, quoted by Tom Francis, described it as 'a monument to churchwardenism at its worst' and as a 'sorry pile of bricks and stucco'.

As a boy, Thomas Francis senior was an organ-blower, and used to tell how, with others, he relieved the tedium of the job behind the scenes by allowing the 'mouse', which indicated the amount of air in the organ bellows, to run completely out before furiously blowing it up again. He was later a member of the choir, and remembered forming part of a deputation to the vicar to claim payment. He told his son that his rabbit fluctuated in fatness according to the state of his choir earnings! Tom Francis's close friend James Drewett, a local builder and property developer, parish and urban district councillor, was an enthusiastic campanologist, and badly wanted Tom to join the bell ringers. One Sunday morning he took Tom up the bell tower and initiated him into the art. Tom recalled it afforded him a chance to climb out on to the top of the tower, from which there was 'a fine view of rural Mitcham' to the south and south-east. Tom was not persuaded to become a bellringer, however, and it was some forty years before he ascended the tower again.

Until 1834 the singing in the parish church had been accompanied by a string band, but in that year the opportunity arose to purchase a secondhand organ for £200 from the Argyle Music Room in London. A further £90 was expended in its removal and installation in the gallery where, as can be seen in an interior view of the church taken by John R. Chart, it unfortunately hid most of the fine west window (Pl.31). The choir sat in seats below the organ. The organist, screened from public view by a curtain, is said to have enjoyed his bread and cheese in privacy during the service. In 1874 alterations were made and the organ was removed to the chancel. At the same time the east window was repositioned at the west end of the church, and a new stained glass window inserted above the altar and reredos. Tom Francis recalled hearing that these and other innovations 'caused feelings' in the parish to 'rise' considerably. A skit expressed in biblical terms was published on the controversy, naming such characters as Daniel the Priest, and Sydney the Scribe (Pl.39).

The oldest part of Mitcham churchyard lies in the immediate vicinity of the church. In 1855 an acre was added towards the north and later, after a Burial Board had been established, the churchyard was extended by a further two acres. The former 'vicar's field', which can be seen in an early 20th-century photograph of the eastern end of the church, was added to the churchyard in 1909 and the extension was consecrated by the bishop (Pl.32). No further extensions being possible, the new London Road cemetery was laid out between the two wars on land in north Mitcham which had previously formed part of Tamworth Farm.

Funerary practices had undergone what Tom Francis called 'a sensible change' by the 1940s.

When dad was a boy, people attended funerals in black mourning cloaks which were worn over the usual clothing, [and] crepe bands were wound round the men's hats. Children carried white, black-bordered handkerchiefs. If they could be afforded, dismally dressed mutes stood at the front door. The undertaker and his mutes wore big sashes of crepe round their hats and down their backs – if it was a child's funeral the undertaker would wear a white hat sash. The undertaker led the procession, and the mourners followed. The coffins, covered by big black palls, were usually carried, but if this involved some distance, then relays of bearers would be arranged. Flower tributes were less numerous and less elaborate than those seen today. The funerals of those who were 'well off' were often elaborate affairs, two or four horses drawing the hearse, covered with palls and carrying plumes on their heads. Of course, the horses were 'all blacks' as well, and high steppers but our local Undertaker had recourse to the black lead brush to put his horse into full mourning! Even then, the local steeds had not the dignity of horses trained and groomed for their special vocation. Their well-groomed skins, their flowing manes, long wavy tails and arched necks gave them an impressive bearing.

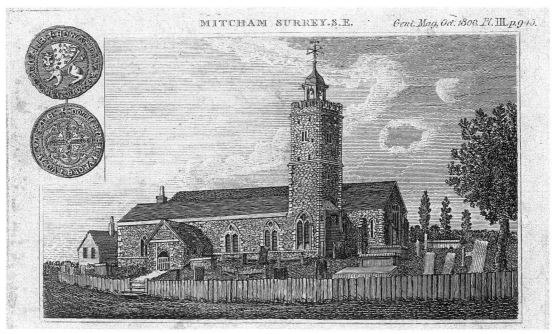

29. Mitcham parish church viewed from the south-east. This engraving was published in the *Gentlemen's Magazine* in October 1800.

30. The west end of Mitcham parish church, as it appeared in 1865, from a field which in 1897 became the site of Lower Mitcham Board School, now known as Benedict Primary School.

31. The interior of Mitcham parish church, before the removal of the organ from beneath the west window in 1875. In this photograph, taken by John R. Chart, one can see the churchwardens' curtained seats beneath the ornately panelled choir gallery. These were removed when the baptistry was formed.

32. The east end of Mitcham parish church, seen from Church Road, *c*.1905. The former 'vicar's field', in the foreground, lay between the church and Love Lane. It was incorporated into the churchyard in 1909.

33. The Rev. Daniel Frederick Wilson M.A. had become vicar of Mitcham in 1859 at the age of twenty-eight. Towards the end of his incumbency in Mitcham – he was vicar for 59 years – he became an honorary canon of Southwark Cathedral.'Tall and dignified', Tom Francis considered him 'exact, prompt and businesslike', although 'hardly a good mixer with his parishioners'. John Marsh Pitt and Tom Francis found themselves sufficiently in favour, however, to be invited to show Easter pictures for the vicar in the parish church on Good Friday for a number of years. The subject was the story of Calvary, told with dissolving views. As a screen a 15 ft. sheet was suspended beneath the chancel arch, and the projector 'used oxy-hydrogen lime light'.

"Our beloved pastor returns to his flock." APRIL 11ᵀᴴ 1878.

34. Collingsby's cartoon showing the vicar's return from a tour of Palestine in 1878. The Rev. Wilson is shown sitting on a triumphal cart, being drawn in procession round Fair Green. Several well-known parishioners accompany him, including George Parker Bidder Q.C. of Ravensbury Park House, and others identifiable from their caricatures reproduced elsewhere in this work.

35. Seen here, on the left, is the Roman Catholic church in Cranmer Road, completed in 1889 to the designs of Robert Masters Chart, architect of the Vestry Hall. In the 1850s, when the congregation was very small, Mass had been held in the coach-house of Elm Lodge, on the opposite side of the Cricket Green, the priest riding over from Norwood on a white horse. Tom Francis understood that in the 'early days of the church' (probably in the 1850s), services had also taken place in rooms at the rear of what in the 1940s was Spence's stationery shop. Pending completion of the new church, services were held in a small brick chapel erected in 1861-62 adjacent to a wooden school building, which stood on the site of the later catholic schools facing the Cricket Green.

36. The Baptist chapel on the Fair Green, photographed by John R. Chart. It stood roughly on land that was later to be occupied by the South Suburban Co-operative Stores. Mr. Poulton, a devout member of the congregation and keeper of a nearby grocery shop, is seen standing by the door. An unpretentious and uninviting building, the chapel was later dismantled and re-erected on the left-hand side of Clarendon Grove. It was eventually superseded by a more commodious chapel erected in London Road, opposite Eagle House.

Village Characters

Tom Francis's early interest in portraiture left a legacy of photographs of village characters which he converted into slides. Many are studies of considerable artistic merit in their own right and, as with most of the collection, Tom's accompanying notes contain a wealth of detail of interest to the local historian.

37.   Old 'Punch' Hugget, who was one of the 'tough guys' of the eighteen eighties. 'Punch' was 'not keen on regular work,' remembered Tom Francis, although he 'could "pick up" a rabbit', and 'used to hawk mandrake root ... It is curious how this type of person, to whom a day's consistent work would be distasteful, will work for days hunting and picking wild fruits and roots for which they may obtain a few coppers.' In a boisterous mood, 'Punch' once bought a bottle of castor oil at the London House stores, 'drank the contents, and chewed the glass bottle up!'

38. 'Mrs. Lossy, mother of Billy, who swept the crossing at the milestone' (ie. at the Cricket Green end of Whitford Lane). Billy 'was a sad cripple,' added Tom Francis, 'and according to the board hanging on his chest he had been struck by lightning when a child.'

39. Sidney Gedge, who lived at Mitcham Hall, a large white house standing back from London Road, near to the site where the Congregational church was erected in 1931. Rather surprisingly, Tom Francis had little to say about Mr. Gedge, apart from commenting that he 'was a great churchman, a friend of the Vicar; a public man; an out and out Tory. He was elected M.P. for Stockport.' In fact Gedge, a Cambridge graduate, was by profession a solicitor and also a licensed preacher in the Southwark diocese. He was churchwarden at Mitcham parish church for many years, and was also active in the work of overseas missions. Gedge's election in 1886 to represent the Stockport constituency was followed, after a break of three years, by his being returned as the member for Walsall in 1895. Gedge, who died in 1923 at the age of 94, was responsible for initiating the development of Mitcham Park in the late 1890s as an estate of somewhat superior houses. This was halted by the First World War, and building work did not recommence until after his death. Tom Francis seems to have been much impressed by Gedge's practice of occasionally cycling to his London office, but was at a loss to give an explanation for the old gentleman's reason for choosing to wear two hats when riding around Mitcham!

40. 'Dummy' Marks had been an employee of Tom Francis's maternal grandfather, but he was an inmate of the Farnborough workhouse when this picture was taken. 'Dummy' used to visit the Francis family from time to time, and young Tom and his brother William found him an amusing old character.

41. Tom Francis's comment on this picture was that 'Patmore was the son of a blind coal-porter who played an ancient organ for a living. His son drove the donkey barrow which carried it. When the donkey retired Patmore wheeled a pram with the organ, and carried on the business when the old porter died. He then found it easier to carry an accordion than to push a "pram". He sometimes "obliged" at mission meetings – *Oh, that will be glory, glory for me* and *Tell Mother I'll be there* were favourites. For the look of things he had a sheet of music in front of him, though it was generally agreed it was useless to him.'

42. This photograph of Widow Bignall was given to Tom Francis by R. M. Jones, who had used the portrait to illustrate an article which he had published. Tom's note accompanying the slide describes Mrs. Bignall as 'a dignified, clever basketmaker. The picture shows her stripping willow, holding it between her teeth. She told me', wrote Tom, 'that she had worn her teeth down and one had then become loose, but she had "wired it in". Tom Sherman, the old cricketer and rough bat maker, supplied her sometimes with willow. She was 88.'

43. Road-widening south of the Cricket Green in the 1950s removed all trace of Westhalls, the old grocer's shop (later Stevenson and Rush) where Tom Francis understood Mitcham's first post office had been located. A second early post office was in a small shop near Mitcham station. This photograph of a group of postmen was taken early one morning before breakfast, and is complete apart from one absentee – George Bennett (*see* Pl.61). Miss Hayward, whose father had served as postmaster, seems to have been the postmistress at the time, and the group comprised: *(Back row)* Hayward junr., Wilkes, 'Tiggy' Croftus. *(Front row)* Webster, Harry Quinby, Hines, H. Neal (in 'civies'), Tommy Turner and Dunstan. Several of the men wear long service stripes. Within a few years the post office was moved to a new building erected next to Sayers' builders office and yard in London Road, but Tom Francis says this was looked upon as inconvenient by the staff. Some thirty years later the post office was relocated on the ground floor of a new telephone exchange building erected by the G.P.O. in London Road, just to the south of the Fair Green.

44. 'Old Wallis', a shoe repairer employed by Thomas Francis senior. Tom and his brother found that Wallis, who in his younger days had been a poacher, and then found employment as a gamekeeper, needed little prompting to recount stories of his long life. One day at Saffron Walden fair he had been persuaded to 'take the Queen's shilling', and went home with the ribbons in his hat. His wife was furious when she discovered what he had done, tore the ribbons out, and marched off to London with Wallis, where presumably she was confident the authorities would be unable to catch him. 'Anyway,' said Tom, 'the Queen never found her soldier!'

45. Charlie Price – 'Nogo' to most of his contemporaries, had worked as a colour boy at Harvey and Knights' floor-cloth factory in Morden Road. 'He never stuck at a job for long, but proved a good hand with a pick on road repairs. He was also a jobbing gardener.' On one occasion Price was accused of attempting to hang himself, which Tom Francis doubted, and accordingly spoke for him at Croydon Court. 'On the Magistrate inviting him to speak, "Nogo" assured him that 'Mr. Francis had spoke the truth and it wouldn't occur again!'

46. A lavender seller. Lavender, for which Mitcham was world famous, at least until the early years of this century, is in full bloom in early August, and was sold in bundles at fair time by gypsies, who hawked it around the streets. Mrs. Sparrowhawk, one of a well-known Mitcham family of Romany stock, was a familiar figure with her black hair, brown face and white teeth, and gave Tom Francis the words of the cry: Who'll buy my Mitcham lavender?/It makes your handkercher so nice./ Who'll buy my blooming lavender?/Sixteen branches for a penny!

47. Two Gallician gypsy boys, members of a 'tribe' of these people who came to England, en route to the United States of America. Whilst in Mitcham they camped in a field near Willow Cottage at Beddington Corner, where they posed as skilled tinkers and repaired copper utensils. One of the girls, daughter of the leader of the band, died whilst they were there, and was buried in Mitcham churchyard with a most elaborate funeral. 'The usual funeral sightseers were increased by a crowd of the local curious', said Tom Francis, and 'extravagant tales were told of the number of solid gold and silver coins which decorated the body of the deceased girl.' Tom thought the Gallicians 'a picturesque crowd', but admitted 'the neighbourhood was not sorry when they moved on'.

48. J. Schneider was turncock for the Metropolitan Water Board, and attended all the fires in Mitcham. He was also an efficient honorary secretary of the Mitcham, Tooting and Balham Horticultural Society. Thomas Francis senior was largely responsible for the society's first open air summer flower show at Mitcham, which was held in a tent in London House meadow, or 'Raleigh's Field', at the corner of Whitford Lane and the Fair Green. The opening ceremony was performed by the Lord Lieutenant of Surrey. The Society's autumn show, principally of fruit, chrysanthemums and dahlias, was held at Tooting.

49.   Men from the Holborn Union workhouse in
Western Road hawking bundles of firewood, which
had been chopped and tied by the inmates.
Foundation stones of the workhouse were laid on
behalf of the Guardians of the Poor of the Holborn
Union in 1885, the buildings being completed the
following year. Accommodation was provided for
1,000 paupers. From 1916 to 1919 the workhouse
was used as a military hospital, and at the
invitation of the commanding officer, Tom Francis
occasionally acted as projectionist for visiting
experts invited to give 'entertaining' lectures,
illustrated with slides, to the convalescent troops
assembled in the large dining hall. The workhouse
buildings were finally used as factory units on what
was known as the James Estate.

50.   Billy Sams, at one time the town crier, lived in
Western Road, next to what Tom Francis knew as
'Trott's shop' – a property long since cleared away.
Sams was a cobbler, and 'raised his garden to
screen his shop from the pathway'. He almost
always wore a top hat, a fashion favoured by most
of the men of his generation. He died in 1880.

51. Old Tom Sherman who, like his father, was a cricketer of renown. Both played for Mitcham and Surrey. Later Tom umpired for the 'Old Buffer's Cricket Club', who played their matches on the part of the Cricket Green opposite their headquarters, the old *Britannia* public house on The Causeway. This is now a private house, 40 Cricket Green. The name of the club was inspired by Fred Gale of Wykeham Cottage, Commonside East, who wrote on cricketing topics under the pseudonym of 'The Old Buffer' in *Bailey's Magazine*. Sherman used to fashion rough cricket bats out of local willow for the village boys – 'handle and blade in one piece ... clumsy and inartistic', according to Tom Francis.

52. An old milkman, with his yoke and cans. These were days when it was not unknown for unscrupulous dairymen to water their milk, and Tom Francis recalled that this particular old fellow would become very annoyed when boys taunted him with shouts of 'Sky Blue!'. Like several of the village cowkeepers at this time, he tended cattle turned out to graze on the Common. The practice, a very ancient one, vigorously defended by those who laid claim to grazing rights, was brought to an end by the Common Conservators.

53. A group of village children, photographed *c.*1889.

54. Mr. Hudson and his son, outside Lorne Villa, which adjoined Berkeley Place near the junction of today's Baron Grove with London Road. Hudson set up a watch repair shop here, moving later to a small shop opposite the butchers in Lower Mitcham. Subsequently he moved to the High Street, Upper Mitcham (immediately to the north of Fair Green) where, according to Tom Francis, writing in 1945, 'Mrs. Hudson (daughter-in-law) still carries on'.

55. A 'road-up' flag-signaller photographed by Tom Francis opposite London House during the laying of the branch tramline from Fair Green to the *White Hart* in about 1910.

56. Loafers in the trough of the village pump at the Fair Green – 'not an unusual sight', recalled Tom Francis. This photograph, which is undated, was obviously taken well before 1898, by which time the pump had been replaced by the present clock tower.

The Collingsby Cartoons

Collingsby, or 'Mug' as he signed himself, was a resident of Mitcham with a reputation as a clever artist and the ability to characterise in pen and ink sketches. A series of his cartoons was exhibited by Thomas Francis senior in a glass case outside the London House stores in 1879. The subjects were local, the captions Victorian, and the humour often crude, but Collingsby's portraits were considered very clever at the time, creating great interest and amusement. Tom Francis acquired a large number of them and had several copied and made into slides. A few have been included elsewhere in this selection from Tom's collection, but the following seem worth reproduction in a group of their own.

57.   The first in this small selection of Collingsby's studies is of Samuel Bateman, described by Tom Francis as 'the village poet', and as 'a sedate and important person ... with a strange objection to seeing himself in a mirror'. The subjects Bateman chose for his rhymes were local topics, such as *The Dumb Bells of Mitcham* when the parish church bells ceased to be rung whilst a solution was found to a dispute with the vicar over the ringers' remuneration, and the river – *Down by the Wandle's wandering stream, there on the banks now let me dream*. Some of his poems were published in a local paper, *The Advertiser*, their subjects being *The New Directory, The Royal Jubilee Bullock, The Revival of the Old Parish Clock*, and *Farewell to French Pennies*. To one of these compositions the editor · appended the following rhyming comment:
'We thank the Lord for his splendid verses/He has our thanks and not our curses/But what it means and is all about/ Is what we never shall find out.'

"I'M (POET
DO YOU KNOW IT ?"

58. In this cartoon by Collingsby we see the vicar, Daniel Wilson, shown with a very different local character, Billy Ramsey, a jobbing gardener. Unfortunately today we can only guess at the intended innuendo, and the significance of their portrayal in front of the National Schools building. Tom commented that Ramsey 'was credited with possessing two sizes in spades, one for piece work, and the other for employment by the hour'. His trade sign, displayed on his cottage wall, bore the quaint legend 'Going Out Gardening Done Here'. Tom was prompted by reminiscences of Billy Ramsey to recall the story of another old Mitcham gardener who for some reason refused to drink his beer except from an earthenware flowerpot, in which the hole had of course to be plugged with a cork.

59. A Valentine Day skit by Collingsby, purporting to represent the batch of cards from satisfied customers received at London House by Thomas Francis senior (seen to the right). Exaggeration or not, it does record the fact that so many Valentines came through the post (not to Thomas Francis, his son was at pains to make clear) that a postman had to use a perambulator to carry them! Two of the postmen portrayed with their three-wheeler 'prams' in this cartoon are George Bennett and Harry Quinby.

SAINT VALENTINE'S DAY. 1878.
A FEW VALENTINES SENT BY REGULAR CUSTOMERS TO "LONDON HOUSE".

60. The next slide (one of a pair) was a composite of 10 caricatures taken from a large cartoon by Collingsby entitled 'Merrie Mitcham'. The border consisted of slogans and pronouncements emphasising the first class value to be obtained at London House stores. The characters portrayed are – Church: The vicar, the Rev. D. F. Wilson; Harmony: The bandmaster of the Holborn School boys' band. His pride in his boys was very evident when he led the band in processions; Cricket: James Southerton, an outstanding slow bowler and landlord of *The Cricketers*, who played for England both at home and in Australia, as well as for Surrey and Mitcham. Tom and his friends playing on the Green were thrilled when Southerton would bowl a few balls down to them. He was buried in Mitcham churchyard, where his headstone is incised with a suitable epitaph telling of his cricketing achievements and genial disposition; Experience: John Bowyer, another Mitcham cricketer of renown, depicted as if in his second childhood; Seeds: John R. Chart, sitting on a camera; Uncle: James Mouland, who kept the pawnbroker's shop at the corner of Sibthorpe Road, and also the jeweller's a few doors away. He specialised in men's working boots, and thus came into business rivalry with London House. His shop sign was a beehive. Mouland was a persistent advertiser, and in one of his ventures used a little two-wheeled pony cart with boards on three sides displaying placards. The village lads enjoyed it thoroughly – it was a target asking for brickbats; Pills: A local doctor, who objected strongly to being caricatured; Temperance: Thomas Francis senior; Official: The village postmaster, H. W. Hayward. His office in the late 1870s was in a small shop down by Mitcham station; Crichton: Thomas Compton, schoolmaster at the National School.

61. The second of the two slides showing an assembly of caricatures of Mitcham worthies. Poesy: Samuel Bateman, the village poet; Laity: William Harwood. He was the Schools Officer; Activity: George Bennett, a postman, born 18 November 1851. Besides being a postman George kept the Little Wonder stationery, tobacco and confectionery shop at Fair Green. He also caned chairs, did a bit of photography, and repaired bicycles. In his leisure time George 'did a bit of running in local sports', and was a sergeant in the Volunteers. On his retirement from the postal service, which he had joined 'at 5.30 a.m. November 18th 1869' and left after 48 years service 'at 7.30 p.m. November 17th 1917' George Bennett became a beekeeper, partly because he had been informed that bee stings were a cure for rheumatism. According to George, the cure worked. At 95 years of age he was still active, exhibiting honey, wax and bee material at local shows. Tom Francis observed that it either said much for the cartoonist's ability that people who knew George Bennett in the 1940s could still recognise him in a drawing made some sixty years before, or else 'said more' for the virility and vigour of the veteran himself; Toil: Billy Ramsey, the jobbing gardener; Figs: Storell, a typical country grocer who had a small shop facing Lower Green West, on the site of Wotton Cottage, a house erected on the Worsfold estate; Larnin [sic]: Dr. William Smith of Mitcham Lodge College; Grace: Mr. McLachlan, who lived in Chestnut Cottage, facing the Cricket Green. Mrs. McLachlan was a performer on the piano and a teacher of music; Humility: A scripture reader, popularly known as 'Holy Joe'; Cupid: Samuel Love, proprietor of the draper's shop on Fair Green, where later Davey and Hart's offices were built. Love acted as collector of funds for the purchase and erection of the clock tower on Fair Green to commemorate Queen Victoria's Diamond Jubilee in 1897. On retiring from the drapery trade, he became the Mitcham rate collector, and lived at 13 Glebe Villas, in London Road. Love had a famous talking cockatoo, whose profile in Tom Francis's opinion much resembled that of its master. Munday, Samuel Love's shop assistant, carried on as a men's outfitter in one of the shops later demolished to provide a site for the present Lloyd's Bank; Collingsby: 'Mug' the artist. Tom Francis admitted he knew little about Collingsby, except that he was 'a very clever chap' and always seemed glad to earn a few shillings by his drawings. He specialised in 'life size' portraits executed in crayon.

Shops and Shopping

Thomas Francis senior was characterised by his son as 'a stout-hearted draper, trained in the school of experience. In the days prior to Carter Paterson's extensive service, Dad carried a large black linen sack on his journeys to London and frequently brought it home by rail filled to capacity, as much as he could carry.' It was not unknown for him to be challenged by the ticket collectors for payment of excess luggage. Looking back, Tom Francis used to comment that prices seemed to have been 'incredibly low – women's black stockings 3¾d. a pair, calico 1½d. a yard, flannel 5¼d. and 6¼d. a yard'. He recalled that 'Red flannel was a basic speciality. And when women discarded red flannel petticoats Dad thought the end had come!' As we have already seen, Thomas Francis and his wife Eliza had been assistants in London House since the early 1860s, when the shop was in the hands of George Pitt and, their son tells us, by 1869 'carried on the business on their own behalf'. Tom himself was born over the shop, and started work there in 1886. His memories of 'behind the scenes' provide us with intriguing insights into the running of what had undoubtedly become a modestly prosperous commercial enterprise by the closing years of the Victorian era.

In the earliest surviving photograph of the shop, taken c.1868, one can see a lean-to at the side, which extended the display area (Pl.62). This was later demolished and replaced with a more substantial brick building, for some reason known as the 'Rod in Pickle'. Being lit by a glass skylight, it was not very secure, and burglars found their way in on at least one occasion. In the photograph behind the main shop-blind one can just see what was a confectioner's shop in the 1860s, and beyond that two timber-framed weatherboard cottages where in Tom's early days lived the Misses Wasley and the Misses Beaman, who ran a little school. Three brick-built shops – Russell the jeweller, Hunt the greengrocer and Birch the butcher – replaced the wooden cottages, and beyond them came Raleigh Gardens, so named because the land had once been owned by Elizabeth, née Throckmorton, who married Sir Walter.

In 1879 the former confectioner's shop and house (it had subsequently become a printer's) was bought by the proprietors of London House. The stores could now be extended, and a new shop front was installed, uniting both premises. In 1901 Francis's ironmongery shop and dwelling house was built, and shortly afterwards a lock-up drapery shop took the place of the 'Rod in Pickle' (Pl.63). Years later new windows to the outfitting and shoe departments were installed by Parnells, creating the façade of 280-6 London Road which was to remain substantially unaltered until the shop was demolished in the 1950s.

Before 1879 the family's living room, the shop parlour, was three or four steps up from the shop itself. The floor was later lowered to the level of the shop, although this was to the detriment of the cellarage below. The parlour was used by the Francis children, and for meals on Sundays, but the rest of the domestic accommodation was upstairs, mainly towards the front of the house. The 'french windows' to the principal room on the first floor opened onto a balcony, which was surrounded by iron railings, and therefore a safe vantage point from which to watch the traffic on Epsom race days.

In the 1870s bees found their way into the top bedroom, to the great annoyance of the 'mother's help' employed by the Francises. They eventually became such a nuisance that something had to be done, and when the floor boards were lifted over 60lbs. of honey were discovered, some quite old and very dark, but the rest recent. This was displayed in the shop window (Tom Francis does not say whether or not it was offered for sale). At the time the main trading opposition to London House came from James Mouland, proprietor of a pawnbroking firm trading from a shop known as The Beehive in the High Street, Upper Mitcham. Never one to miss an opportunity, Thomas Francis senior had a notice prepared on which was written 'Uncle may have the Beehive, but we'll be content with the honey'.

London House was, or at least claimed to be, a pioneer in several marketing stratagems, one of which was the production of presentation calendars, given to favoured customers. The first was a localised version of a well-known popular calendar, but London House soon produced its own in the form of a card printed on both sides and headed with an engraving of the shop. The goods and prices advertised in these early calendars included such items as men's guinea overcoats and black dress coats, men's 8s.6d. side spring boots and women's goat or cloth side spring boots at 6s.6d. Cashmere boots were 2s.6d. a pair, and Paris hats ('toppers') 7s.6d. Children's side springs were 5s.6d., watches could be cleaned for 2s.6d., and the seemingly endless list of sundries included such diverse items as candle snuffers, tea trays and fish hooks. It was emphasised that all goods were marked in plain figures at even prices, and with 'No odd farthing tricks'. The calendars carried a notice for the boot and clothing club, with the promise of interest of 3d. to every shilling, and also announced that a registry was kept for servants. Details of the postal arrangements were given, train times from Mitcham station, and also the times of Samson's City and West End horse buses, which started from the Lower Green. A special feature was made of 'phases of the moon' – an important consideration in those days, when street lighting was very rudimentary. Printing of the calendar was undertaken by E. Field, who until 1879 occupied the premises adjoining London House. (Field moved to Caxton Works, Lower Green, former school premises which later were taken over by Compton and then Mather.)

Another of Thomas Francis's marketing innovations was a 'Prize Week', held for a number of years during the first week in July. Prizes were given to all customers spending five shillings, ten shillings or a guinea, and consisted of teaspoons, metal teapots, china tea services and dinner services. The variety was widened as the years went by. 'Prize week was well advertised, and brought customers from Lower Cheam, Morden, Carshalton and so on. Bill delivering was done by the firm, and was much enjoyed by us as boys', said Tom, 'perhaps on account of lunch at a 'pub'.' It was a busy week for the shop assistants, but beer was always handy for the thirsty, and 'strawberries – heaps of em, for the juniors'.

Thomas Francis always employed a boy or two on the staff at London House. Some were indentured and came from the various industrial schools in the neighbourhood, such as Sutton (which Tom Francis referred to as 'the linger or die'), Anerley, and St George's at Mitcham. On leaving they often became postmen, policemen, soldiers or sailors, the uniform seeming to be an attraction. Owing to the quantity of stock displayed outside the shop, employment of 'a boy outside' was a necessary precaution against pilfering. During a particularly cold spell, one enterprising lad contrived to keep himself warm with a bonfire on the pavement, until stopped by the police.

Most of the old shops in Mitcham at this time were fitted with stall boards and shutters, some fifty or so in the case of London House, all of which had to be barred and bolted at night. 'Even though we might have been closing down at 9 p.m., and on Saturdays at 11 and on busy days nearer midnight, the 'putting up' of 50 shutters engendered a kind of 'fed up' feeling!', remembered Tom.

> Naked gas flares lit the proceedings, always on the flicker and outside sometimes blowing out. A splash was made in 1880 with an opal globe over each burner, each one bearing a large black letter F.R.A.N.C.I.S. Not a great success! There were several improved types of burner, and when a pub installed incandescent gas mantles, it appeared almost a miracle of light. We all followed.

At one period powerful 100-200 candle-power paraffin oil lamps were hung at each end of the shop – a 'good light but a great nuisance to me – the filler and trimmer', Tom recollected. The earliest type of domestic mantles sold at London House were of the upright pattern, and cost 2s.6d. each. Inverted mantles came later, to the confusion of many of the store's customers who, with only a meagre education, and that often at Sunday school, asked for either 'converted' or 'unconverted' mantles. The rapidity with which artificial lighting was being improved was one of the wonders of the age, and Thomas Francis senior took his shoemakers to the first Electric Light Exhibition, held at the Crystal Palace.

London House proclaimed in bold letters that it was the 'Shop for everything and everybody' and proudly drew attention to having been established as long ago as 1830.

> Little merchandise came amiss to the counters of London House if an honest penny could be turned: Cap fronts, magnets, beads, gridirons, crinolines, dress suspenders, spectacles, seals, clogs, coral necklaces, poll combs, hair nets, chest protectors, pomatum, perfumes, soap, and even small bottles of castor oil ... Dad was stopped by one of his clients one Sunday who complained sadly of the potency of the innocent looking little bottle of C.O ...'Joe', one of the helpers, came back excitedly from the Fair with a bottle of pomatum, especially cheap and good. He had tried it, and wanted the governor to invest in a lot for sale. But not in the morning! He, Joe, awoke with his hair strongly pasted together.

In the severe winter of 1881, when work stopped on the land and out-of-doors, Mitcham labourers, with their small wages, were soon in want.

> Soup kitchens, robin dinners, and various organisations had to be set going. For a week teas were given in London House garden. Thick chunks of bread and butter and mugs of tea, the guests sitting round a big fire and listening to a nigger with a banjo and songs. The people came in parties of about 30 or so.

Nigger minstrel troops were much in vogue at that time, and one Christmas attraction at London House was a display of 'darkie' pictures in very gay colours, but in what Tom Francis considered 'lowbrow taste'. The scenes, he remembered, 'included "The Darkie's Wedding", the "Crack Trotter", "A Swell sport on a buffalo hunt" and the like'. Clockwork models were another Victorian window attraction, together with toys and, of course, Christmas cards.

62. London House stores in 1868

63. London House stores, *c*.1910.

64. An old wooden house in Christchurch Road, standing opposite the junction of Church Road with Phipps Bridge Road. This had been used as a barn by Jonathan Meadows, a calico bleacher, in the late 18th century, but was in a very dilapidated state towards the end of the Victorian period, when it is said to have acquired the nick-name of 'Rat Castle'. At one time there was a confectioner's shop there, and Tom Francis recalled seeing a notice board inside on which was written: 'Man to man is so unjust/He will not pay when he gets trust./ I've trusted many to my sorrow,/So pay today, and trust tomorrow!' The shop keeper was certainly a cautious man, for when young Tom went in one day

with the intention of buying a bottle of ginger beer, he was told to hand over the money before pulling the cork! The Pickle Ditch, which flowed alongside Phipps Bridge Road (now Liberty Way) turned north at this corner and, after actually flowing beneath the building, meandered alongside Mead, or Brook, Path and watercress beds to join the Wandle by Merton Bridge. In very wet weather, and after severe rain storms, the road in the vicinity of the house was one of the first to flood. This was overcome between the wars by improvements to the system of surface water drainage. The Pickle Ditch had defined the south-eastern and eastern extent of the grounds of Merton Priory, and land on which part of the old precinct walls still survived, alongside the path to just south of Merton Bridge, was purchased by the River Wandle Open Spaces Committee in 1915 and presented to the National Trust.

65. The Broadway Stores, which stood next to the *Old Nag's Head* on the northern side of Upper Green West. Groceries, oil and colour, brooms and brushes were sold along with some items of household ironmongery. The halved olive oil jars mounted on the front of the building at first floor level are interesting – these were the once common shop sign displayed by oil and colour merchants. After the old shop had been demolished, the Fair Green covered market was erected on the site. (This in its turn was cleared away in the 1980s, and the site is traversed by a new road.)

66.   Currell's sweet and greengrocery shop, facing Fair Green. Many of the village shops seemed to be in this type of building, and Tom Francis could recall examples surviving on both sides of the Green in the 1880s and '90s. The plaster rendering on the front elevation probably masked a timber framing, and the date of the building could be 17th century or even earlier.

67.   Collbran's Corner at Fair Green. The pump in the foreground replaced an earlier one in 1865, and was itself superseded by the clock tower and drinking fountain erected in 1898 to commemorate Queen Victoria's Diamond Jubilee. The Salvation Army made the pump its open-air rendezvous, and it was also a rallying point for local orators, politicians and any malcontent who wanted to get something off his chest. The pump raised water from a well beneath the road, and had been an important source of water for the ordinary people of the village. A few of the larger houses at this time still relied on their own wells and pumps, but increasingly connections were being made to the new water mains. The lamp above the pump was an open gas jet, supplied from the Mitcham Gas Light and Coke Company's Works in Merton Lane (now Western Road), which had begun production in 1849.

68. Neddy Collbran outside his butcher's shop at Fair Green. Neddy's father, 'a typical village butcher who operated on an old-type thick wooden chopping block', was the proprietor in Tom Francis's childhood days. It was Thomas Francis senior's custom to buy the weekend joint himself for his family of seven children. 'A fine chunk of meat it was', remembered young Tom, 'real home killed, rich and juicy – none of your frozen anaemic looking stuff, but the real thing, a pleasure to see wheeling backwards and forwards on the old clockwork meat jack. And what dripping and what toast, if you could manage to dip it in the pan for a few minutes on the quiet!' The Collbrans' slaughtering was done in a wooden building to the left of the shop, fitted with wooden trellis over the window apertures to screen the interior from the eyes of inquisitive boys.

69. A general view of the eastern side of Fair Green in about 1870. The Green then was quite open, and at times even had a little grass on which animals might forage. The row of shops remained little changed for many years. Some had bow fronts, and all had small window panes. Tom Francis remembered from his childhood that one had been occupied by Mrs. Mills, 'wife of the village policeman with a gingery beard. She sold greengrocery, – sage, thyme and all that. There was a lovely refreshing smell in the shop. She also kept the good old sweets in glass jars – Black Jacks, Peppermints, Aniseed Balls, Sugar Candy, Coltsfoot Rock, Sugar sticks, Sweet Almonds, Burnt Almonds, Pear Drops, Carraway Comforts, Mottoes, Stick Jaw, Hundreds of Thousands, etc. etc.' In George Bennett's Little Wonder one could buy newspapers, as well as pipes, tobacco and sweets, song sheets 'crude and rude and gaudy', Valentines in season and boat race favours. Others in this row were Ruff's shoe repair shop, Samuel Love's three shops – outfits and drapery – and Sewell's (late Pitman's) boot and shoe store, a grocer's shop, and Lane the harness maker. 'Shopkeepers of the Fair Green were stout Mitcham characters', recalled Tom.

70. Here, in another photograph of *c*.1870, can be seen some of the Fair Green shops in close-up. Robert Rice's Drapery Warehouse later became Samuel Love's, and was at one time *the* drapery store in Mitcham, boasting many 'carriage' customers. The Mitcham Supply stores, to the right, was a grocer's. Tom Francis used to recall that following a fire, during which stock was damaged by water, great slabs of chocolate were sold for a few pence to the village lads, who were not in the least put off by the condition of the wrappers.

71. This photograph completes the record of the old shops on the eastern side of the Fair Green. It was taken from the corner of Whitford Lane, now London Road, and shows the row of venerable elms lining what was then known as Langdale Walk. These trees were severely lopped during the late 1890s on the order, so it was believed, of the chairman of the parish council, Alfred Mizen. His political opponents attempted to stir up local indignation against him for despoiling the trees, which they dubbed 'Clothes Prop Walk'. A clothes line was hung between them bearing a political poster, but Tom Francis was of the opinion that the slogan had little effect when polling day arrived.

72. John R. Chart's seed shop at the corner of the Fair Green and the *Three Kings* pond. The door of the shop had a tinkling bell, and inside the atmosphere was distinctly 'mousey'. There were bins for oats, chaff and dog biscuits, and in the left hand window were displayed sprays of millet, gaily coloured packets of seed, china eggs and a white plaster of Paris horse. 'As children we experienced great joy in making our selection from the gaily pictorial packets of garden seeds done up in penny packets and spread before us by Mrs. John', recalled Tom Francis. The other window showed miniature trusses of hay. The printing on paper bags of flour, and on a frame of photographs, announced that John R. Chart was also a photographer.

73. Old shops and cottages on Commonside West near Cold Blows. (The *Windmill* can just be seen on the left.) Here John ('Jackie') Sanders kept a little shop, selling sweets etc., and repairing boots. Like many of the older men in the village, he was usually to be seen wearing a top hat, especially on Sundays.

74. Shops in London Road, Lower Mitcham, south of the *White Hart*. These shops were of a type common in the village, created by the adaptation of former private houses. According to Tom Francis, there was at one time a toy shop here, and later Sam Turner, the bootmaker, occupied one of them. Sam had the honour of making boots for the Australian cricketers when they visited Mitcham for practice. Around the turn of the century these apparently 18th-century premises were replaced by a new red-brick building, which, during the inter-war years, accommodated the Wandsworth Gas Company showrooms and offices and Robinson's dairy. The National Fire Service took over from the gas company during the Second World War, but the showrooms reverted to their former use once the war was over.

75. Shops in London Road, Lower Mitcham, photographed from opposite the *White Hart*. A notice fixed to the wall of houses on the right (out of the picture) proclaimed that this narrow section of the road south from the Cricket Green was known as 'The Broadway'. The butcher's shop (with a blind) was new when the photograph was taken. Further

down on the same side of the road were several shops which had been built in front of old houses with tiled roofs. Here there was a grocer's, a sweet shop and a shoe repairer's. Years ago this last shop had a verandah extending over the path. The end buildings in the row, coming immediately before the high garden wall of the Manor House, were the mock-Tudor gabled premises of the post office and, finally, the office and yard of Charles Sayers the builder. These had replaced a small bakery and confectioner's and a little bow-fronted shop once belonging to Boys the plumber (an old-time cricketer), where Tom recalled there always seemed to be rolls of lead laid in front.

76. Gulland's, Bryant's, Henty's or Howe's, Corner facing the Cricket Green. (In accordance with village custom, whoever occupied the small cottage in the centre of this photograph gave his name to the corner.) The front room of the cottage was a little confectionery and tobacco shop, entered by two steps down from the pavement outside. The window to the left of the door had a display of pipes and tobacco. This was a 'loafers corner', and one can see clearly the black smudge on the wall where, in Tom Francis's words, 'generations of tired men rested their backs'. To the left is the London and Provincial Bank, its fascia board just visible behind the old elm tree. Before becoming a bank, this had been Summerfield's the tailor, and after that, the offices of the Croydon Rural Sanitary Authority.

77. This photograph of Barclays Bank on the corner of London Road and Lower Green West provides an interesting comparison with the preceding illustration. Observing in his notes that the new bank building hardly fits into the Mitcham landscape, Tom Francis described it as 'Mitcham's first bank', by which he obviously meant the first building specifically designed for the purpose. The adjacent premises, occupied by the London and Provincial Bank, were soon to be demolished and the site used for an extension to Barclays. Lloyds Bank and the Westminster Bank later established branches at Fair Green, which obliged Barclays to open an Upper Mitcham branch. Thomas Francis senior banked with Barclays, and until the Mitcham branch opened he had been obliged to send his son to Croydon by train at least once a week. Tom made the best of these opportunities, and if the visit was on a Thursday he attended the mid-week Society of Friends' meeting before, as he put it, 'finishing at Croydon baths'.

Getting About

Although by the late 1860s the village was served by two railway stations, Mitcham Junction and Mitcham, with a third within easy reach at Tooting Junction, the movement of goods locally was still entirely dependent on horse-drawn vehicles, and most ordinary people had, perforce, to rely on 'shanks's pony'.

The state of the roads at this time is worth comment, and their condition can be judged from a photograph of the *Swan* inn, Upper Mitcham, taken in 1865 (Pl.70). The principal highways were repaired by filling potholes and then covering the surface with flints, which had been dumped in heaps at the roadsides to await being smashed to the required size by stonebreakers wielding long-handled hammers. The broken stones were not rolled in, but were left to be worn down gradually and consolidated by the traffic, so that for weeks after 'repair' the road surfaces were quite rough. The employment of a large roller, pulled by six horses, was a great advance, and later still came the steam roller. Stonebreaking was one of the heavy manual jobs imposed on able-bodied men who sought lodging and food in the workhouses. Mitcham parish workhouse on the Common was closed in 1838, after which local men on relief had to journey to Mayday Road, Croydon, to do their stonebreaking.

No road watering was undertaken by the local authority at this time, and during dry weather dust flew in clouds from the flint surfaces. The situation was often bad enough for occupiers of houses and shops with a road frontage to arrange their own road watering. Thomas Francis senior used to have about 150 yards of Whitford Lane in front of London House watered to lay the dust and save his stock from being spoiled. For the purpose a huge barrel had been mounted on a platform and fitted with a perforated pipe. It was filled from a pump, and would be operated by one of the men employed about the shop as the need arose.

There was no watering of Whitford Lane by the shop staff on race days, for one of London House's best lines was 'Derby veils', which they sold to racegoers. The veils were made from brightly coloured muslin, fitted with elastic at one end for putting on the ladies' hats. Young Tom wasn't sure whether or not the veils had been a London House invention, as was claimed, but they were certainly well worth making, and whilst women assistants were busy cutting and fitting, the men enjoyed chasing after the brakes and coaches. 'Sometimes they stood on the steps of vehicles and sold perhaps 20 veils', Tom recollected, adding that, when proper watering was undertaken by the council, the sales dropped off and 'the game was up'.

Regular watering of the main roads actually commenced about 1890, and at first was paid for by public subscription. Tom Francis junior recalled that he had acted as collector once or twice. Eventually responsibility for watering was accepted by the local highway authority. When the practice of surface dressing with granite chips was adopted far less dust was created, and the problem ceased altogether with the introduction of tar-bound macadam.

In the 1860s the lane leading from Roe Bridge over the river Graveney on the Streatham boundary to Figges Marsh was edged with tall trees (Pl.79). As a result, it was shady during the day, and dark and lonely at night. The photograph shows one of the old gas street lamps which, for economy, were placed in store during the summer months, and were not lit in winter when the moon was full. According to Tom Francis this dark lane was the scene of the silly exploits of 'Spring Heel Jack' who, it was popularly believed, was shod in spring heeled boots which enabled him to take extraordinary leaps, and to appear suddenly from behind the hedgerows, scaring women and young people.

The surface of Streatham Lane, shaded as it was by trees, was notoriously slow to dry, and therefore often muddy. The situation was not improved by its being crossed near Figges Marsh by the Little Graveney, flowing from Pollards Hill. A culvert took the water under the road, but after periods of heavy rainfall there was tendency to flooding.

The southern margin of the Cricket Green was similarly vulnerable, and here the name of the 'Causeway' (usually corrupted to 'Causey' by local people) almost certainly arose because at some time the road had been raised a little above the low-lying ground on either side (Pl.80). A ditch flowing in a north-westerly direction alongside Cranmer Road, and now piped underground, seems to have passed behind a row of cottages fronting the highway, and the area must always have tended to be boggy. Tom Francis noted that in the early days of cricket the Green had needed faggot draining to improve matters.

In an early wet-plate photograph of the Lower Green, dating from *c.* 1865, one can see one of Mitcham's horse buses outside the *Cricketers* (Pl.80). Phillip Samson, the bus proprietor, lived in the house next to the accessway leading to the *White Hart* yard. From the first floor window he had a good view of his bus yard behind the house, and according to Tom Francis the old man had a mirror fixed to the wall so that he could see his buses whilst lying in his bed. Tom had been told that Samson had been a stagecoach driver on the route from London via Harwich and Yarmouth to Norwich. The Mitcham buses were drawn by two or three horses, and each carried a guard complete with horn. Walter Samson, one of the sons, drove the principal bus – the 9 o'clock to the City – which clattered through the village to the accompaniment of blasts on the horn. The other route was to the West End. Before the opening of the Wimbledon to Croydon railway in 1855, another bus provided the only public conveyance from Mitcham to Croydon station.

Tom Francis recalled that in his youth a seat by the coachman was an envied position, and that on wet days straw was strewn on the floor inside. The top of these buses was, of course, open to the weather, and waterproof aprons were supplied to the passengers. In rough weather gentlemen were expected to give up the inside seats to ladies, whilst they braved the elements outside. In foggy weather, the buses carried flaming torches.

The fares of 1s. single each way or 1s.6d. return were not considered excessive, and the buses had their regular patrons. Fred Gale of Wykeham Cottage (later known as The Croft), Commonside East, was amongst them. On one occasion, striding across Figges Marsh, he overtook the bus. The driver drew up for him but, no doubt to the amusement of the other passengers, Fred declined with a 'Not today, thanks, Walter, I'm in a hurry!'.

Samson also contracted to supply horses for the Mitcham fire engine *Caesar*, and after the firemen had answered the summons to the station, located within the present Vestry Hall, it was not unknown for them to have to wait for a bus or cab to return to the yard. A hustle then ensued to unhitch the horses and harness them to the fire engine.

The end of the horse buses came with the arrival of a new form of public transport, the electric tramcar. These first ran through Mitcham from Tooting Junction, and then across the Common to Croydon, in 1906. Some two years later a branch line was laid down from Fair Green to the Lower Green (Pl.84). This short section was not a great success, and it was the first to be dismantled when the whole system was cleared away and trolley buses substituted in the 1930s. Most of the rails were taken up in the 1940s for resmelting as part of the war effort.

Traffic passing through Mitcham in the late 19th century may not have been as heavy as that today, but it certainly did not lack variety. From their vantage point of the first floor windows of London House the Francis family were well able to watch the traffic along Whitford Lane, particularly colourful during the race weeks at Epsom, when crowds of Londoners made their way through Mitcham. 'Besides coaches, drags, and buses', Tom recalled, 'there were heavy open landaus drawn by two or four horses with postillions. Riders such as Sir John Bennett, a shrinking figure with white locks waving over his shoulders, and Edward, Prince of Wales, with his company.' The royal party changed horses either at the *King's Head* or an inn in Merton, but, owing to certain insults received from crowds who had gathered to watch, the Prince is said to have taken to travelling by train.

It was not only the racegoers who provided entertainment for those with time to watch. Early motorcars were a great sensation, and when one passed the shop the signal was given, and there would be a rush to the doorway by both customers and assistants eager to witness the wonderful invention travelling along Whitford Lane under its own power. Gypsy caravans with a number of spare horses in tow were no uncommon sight, and there were travelling showmen's vans and circuses making their way back to London and their winter quarters. Cages of wild animals, lumbering elephants, and camels and zebra making their own pace were a source of great delight to the Francis children, although to their dismay they often passed by in the small hours of the morning, before the family were out and about.

In the early days this kaleidoscopic show was further enriched by the sight of flocks of sheep and goats, herds of cattle, horses and even flocks of gaggling geese passing by on their way to the London markets. 'Marching soldiers came through for exercise, and companies of mounted troops with their baggage waggons, which sometimes pulled up on the Cricket Green whilst the men found billets for the night in the village pubs and stabled their horses where they could.'

Then there were the eccentrics, such as a fellow en route for Brighton balancing a two-gallon stone bottle on his head, or another wheeling a barrow with the same destination in mind. Cycles of all description passed by, including penny-farthings, the 'Otto' and the 'facile', the 'sociable' with seats side by side, one-wheel machines ridden by trick cyclists, bikes with six men riding tandem, and one with many wheels, ridden by eight or ten blind men behind one sighted companion who did the steering. The list seems endless. Club cycling was 'all the rage', the members taking themselves very seriously, often sporting a uniform of knickers buttoned below the knee, jackets or tunics with braided decoration over the chest, and polo hats which Tom Francis thought were like 'salad baskets in reverse'. A keen cyclist himself in his early days, Tom and his friends, Alfred and Ernest Mizen and James Drewett, made several trips to Brighton in the 1890s, and he was proud of having completed a round trip of 90 miles over the Hog's Back to Farnham and back via Godalming and Dorking on old Surrey roads that were still little more than rough gravel tracks.

78.   London Road and the *Swan* inn, photographed in 1865. A small triangular fragment of Figges Marsh, taken for road widening many years ago, can be seen on the left.

79.   Streatham Lane in 1865. On the left can be seen the fence surrounding the grounds of Gorringe Park, whilst to the right is farmland. Until 1900 this view remained much the same. James Pascall's sweet factory, famous for its chocolates and sugar confectionery, was then built on the land to the right, by which time Gorringe Park had begun to be sub-divided for development as housing estates whilst the mansion had become an orphanage.

80. A general view of The Causeway, overlooking the Cricket Green, taken c.1870. During the Second World War, as part of the 'Dig for Victory' campaign, the Green opposite the police station was dug up for allotment gardens, and was not returned to grass until some years after the War had ended.

81. In the more remote parts of the parish, typically towards Pollards Hill, lanes and bridleways could become almost impassable in winter. Although Tom Francis did not locate this photograph precisely in his lecture notes, it was probably taken near Lonesome, towards Streatham Vale, where a combination of a clay subsoil and surface water running off the higher ground turned the 'road' into this morass.

82. Cold Blows, the path leading from the Cricket Green to Commonside West. The dogs in the picture belonged to Sir Cato Worsfold of Hall Place, who generally owned one or two examples of unusual breeds. A photograph taken of the path today from the same point would differ very little from this view, which was probably taken shortly before 1900. In Tom Francis's opinion, 'The reason for its name is obvious – the east wind blows through it'. Although he does not comment on the origin of the path, it seems likely that it is actually of great antiquity, for it provides a direct connection between what must have been an early focus of settlement around the church and the former east common field of the medieval village. Tom Francis commented that, when the picture was taken, 'the path on both sides was flanked by gardens and meadow land', but half a century later 'roads running from London Road, *viz.* Langdale Avenue, Albert Road, Whitford Gardens end at the "Blows", and on the other side is Cumberland House built by Sir Isaac Wilson, and the *News of the World* sports ground.' For some reason towards the end of the 19th century Cold Blows was renamed St Mary's Avenue, perhaps inspired by the name Robert Masters Chart had given to his new house overlooking the Cricket Green. Objections were raised and, on a proposition by a Mr. C. W. Benger, it was agreed that the old name be restored.

83.   A wet-plate photograph of *c*.1865, showing the old *Cricketers*' public house and, outside, one of Phillip Samson's horse buses about to depart for the City. The bus yard lay off Lower Green West, and was entered through gates to the right of the cottages visible in the background of the photograph. After the horse bus service ceased, the yard was used by the urban district and later the borough council as a highways depot, and during the Second World War it was utilised by the National Fire Service.

84. Tramlines being laid in Whitford Lane outside London House in about 1908. The terminus for this short branch line from the Upper Green was opposite the *King's Head* (now known as the *Burn Bullock*).

85. In the centre of this photograph, dated *c*.1880, is the house at Fair Green which, in Tom Francis's boyhood, was the residence of Frederick Samson, veterinary surgeon and proprietor of Samson's forge. Frederick was one of the sons of Phillip Samson, the horse bus proprietor. His brothers were Walter, who drove the buses, and Phillip junior, landlord of the *King's Head* and proprietor of a cab yard in the rear. Fred, whose high pitched voice had earned him the nickname 'Squeaker', was a horseman of local fame, and hunted with the Surrey Staghounds. The hunt sometimes came through Mitcham in pursuit of its quarry, and on one occasion a stag was cornered beneath one of the railway bridges. In winter, when the snow was thick enough, Fred Samson was to be seen driving through Mitcham on a sledge. The road to the side of the house led to his yard; above the entrance was an arched notice board, in the centre of which was a horse's skull. The old house was eventually pulled down to make room for Samson's new red-brick house, which was built on the former yard and garden. A restaurant now covers the front garden, but the house can still be seen behind.

86. Reliance on horses and horse-drawn vehicles meant that many Mitcham people were employed in trades associated with their care and maintenance. Samson the vet and farrier we have met. One or two others like William Kent, seen here at work in his smithy in Sibthorpe Road, also found a place in Tom Francis's collection of slides.

87. Kenward's smithy in London Road, Upper Mitcham.

88. A small saddler's shop, known as 'Beanettes', in Lower Mitcham, roughly opposite the junction of Baron Grove with London Road. The photograph dates from *c.*1869, and a few years later a saddler's was opened opposite the *King's Head* by a man called Leach. Mitcham at this time had yet another harness and saddle maker at Fair Green – Abner Lane – a well-known village 'character' whom Tom Francis described as 'tough, virile and independent'.

89. An 'Otto' cycle, as ridden by George F. Linney, superintendent of the Saffron Walden school, which Tom Francis attended.

90. Whitford Lane in winter, looking north towards Fair Green from outside London House. This photograph was taken sometime prior to 1905, when the stables and wall of Elmwood abutting Whitford Lane were demolished.

91. Whitford Lane had been known as 'the village wash-way' in the 18th century on account of a stream which crossed it from the direction of the *Three Kings* pond. A culvert had been constructed beneath the road years before Tom Francis's time but Mitcham retained one ford which crossed the Wandle near the Watermeads, until the 20th century. It can be seen to the right in this photograph, taken by Tom Francis with his Freud camera 'at about 8 o'clock one morning in March after a slight fall of snow'. Although the date is not stated, the picture was probably taken *c.*1900.

Houses and Cottages

In his *Greater London*, published in 1884, Edward Walford observed that in Mitcham 'Many old Mansions, with wrought iron gates and cedars still standing, attest that the place in former times was inhabited by not a few of the wealthier class.' Although not many of Mitcham's larger houses appear in Tom Francis's collection of slides, we are given rare glimpses of some of the humbler dwellings in the village.

92.   One of Mitcham's largest houses, the Canons, off Madeira Road, was named after the canons of the Augustinian priory of St Mary Overie at Southwark, to whom the site was given by the villagers of Mitcham in the 12th century. The present house had been built in 1680, and as late as the 1940s the grounds still boasted several fine and exotic trees, including a cedar of Lebanon, a tulip tree, a golden chestnut, an evergreen oak and a deciduous swamp cypress. The fish pond predates the Dissolution, as does the pigeon house, which is probably the oldest complete building in Mitcham. Constructed of brick and chalk blocks, in one of which the date MDXI is inscribed, it contains some 400 nesting places. The estate was purchased by the Corporation of Mitcham in 1939, since when the house and grounds have been maintained for public recreational purposes.

93. Cranmers, the Rectory, or Mitcham Villa, was set back from Carshalton Road and was named after the family of that name, descended from Robert Cranmer, an East India merchant, who purchased the estate in 1656. The house was pulled down in 1928 to make way for the Wilson Hospital. The magnificent timber-framed and weatherboarded tithe barn, which stood close by, was demolished at the same time. Although the passing of these old buildings was mourned by many, the new hospital was a tremendous boon to the community. When Tom Francis was young the nearest hospital facilities to Mitcham had been at Croydon, and he recalled that accident cases, if they could not afford transport by cab, were usually 'trundled over on a police stretcher on wheels, bumped across the Common, whatever their trouble'.

94. Elmwood, or The Firs, as older residents of Mitcham, including Tom Francis's parents knew it, lay behind the high wall opposite London House in Whitford Lane, and for that reason it featured rather prominently in his collection of slides. In the days when it had been occupied by Mrs. Daun, school treats were held in the meadows adjoining the gardens. These were great events, with music by the Holborn Schools Band, balloons, races, scrambles for sweets, and an outdoor tea. Sometimes there were even fireworks!

95. The stable buildings of Elmwood, photographed in 1903 from the Fair Green. The brick wall continued down Whitford Lane, and opposite London House (just visible to the right) it was greatly increased in height. Then came a tarred wooden fence and elm and chestnut trees, which gave a rural touch. At the far end, to the south, lay the Cricket Green. The impression that one was in the depths of the country must have been heightened by the song of the nightingales, which Tom Francis could just remember being common on summer evenings in the 1870s. The wooden gates to the Elmwood estate were on the Fair Green boundary, with, to their right, the stables and house of the coachman. The coachman in Tom Francis's boyhood was a Liberal. At the time of an election his boss, a Tory, brought out the party's ribbons and decorated the horse, then the whip, and finally produced a Tory rosette for the coachman. 'No,' said the man, 'the horse is yours, sir, and so is the whip, but I am not.' Elmwood was pulled down around 1906, and what had once been a renowned botanical garden, complete with ornamental waters, was destroyed, and Langdale Avenue and its housing plots laid out across it. The rest of the grounds and adjacent meadowland disappeared under Whitford Gardens and Elmwood and Albert Roads. In the process of redevelopment Whitford Lane was widened and a terrace of shops erected from Fair Green as far as London House.

96. A rather forlorn view of the Elmwood estate during redevelopment, taken some time after 1906, when the tramlines were laid down. The stables and coach house have gone, but part of the garden wall alongside Langdale Walk remains, as do the ruins of the gazebo, or summer house, from which in former days residents of the house could sit and enjoy views across the Common to the distant Surrey hills. In the final years of the estate the gazebo had been relegated to use as an apple store.

97. The date of at least part of the wall which surrounded the grounds of Elmwood was indicated by '1664', cut in the brickwork forming what would appear to have been the pediment of a long-blocked doorway. The wall was pulled down when the Fair Green Wesleyan Methodist church was built in 1908-9. This was destroyed by a landmine dropped by German aircraft on 19 September 1940. Tom Francis recalled that for some time the plot adjoining the church was advertised as suitable for the erection of a cinema. No buyer came forth, and eventually shops were built instead.

98. Houses on the Lower Green in 1870, seen from the corner by the *King's Head*. The old Birches, demolished later to provide a site for the present Birches, built by Sir Isaac Wilson, can be seen on the left. The White House (or Ramornie), The Chestnuts, and the pair of early Victorian 'semis' still survive after 130 years, although the latter are somewhat altered. Beyond, to the right, can be seen various smaller houses, dating mostly from the 18th century, which were cleared to make way for newer buildings including Robert Masters Chart's house, St Mary's, and the Methodist church of 1877, which Chart also designed.

99. A mid-18th century-red-brick house known as St George's, which stood on the road leading from Commonside East towards the *Horse and Groom* at the corner of what is now Manor Road and Tamworth Lane. When showing this slide Tom Francis used to comment that there were at one time several examples of this type of house, brick-built, three-storeyed but not very deep, to be seen in Mitcham. One in Willow Lane had once been occupied by the proprietor of a calico bleaching and printing works, and another had stood near the *Three Kings* public house.

100. Vine House, Lower Green West (seen here on the extreme right), was described by Tom Francis as an 'old Tudor House later made into two'. Haydon, a local builder and decorator, and his family lived here about 1890. The *Victoria County History of Surrey*, published in 1912, refers to what it calls 'Vine Cottage' as 'The oldest house in the parish ... a small brick building – externally washed over with a yellow wash – with a tile roof standing at the north-west corner of Lower Green West. It is two stories high, with attics in the roof, and has angles emphasised by brick quoins of slight projection.' The house was certainly picturesque, and attracted the attention of a number of local artists, including a Mr. Crawford, who presented a painting of it to Mitcham Civic Society. Another picture by Mrs. Moberley, was purchased by Mitcham Borough Council with about fifty others which were hung in the committee rooms and corridors of the Town Hall. 'Years ago,' Tom Francis recorded in his lecture notes, 'in making excavations in the grounds, a skeleton was unearthed ... It was said that the bones were those of a soldier, some said a Colonel of Oliver Cromwell's army.' Apart from adding that the bones were 'reburied in Mitcham churchyard' and that this 'was a picturesque bit of information', he had nothing else to say on the matter. One is left to speculate on what might have been the evidence which led to the identification and, if it was correct, who the officer might have been. Tom concluded his note on the house with the bluntly pragmatic observation that, 'The old house had lived its life, was worn out and was pulled down'.

101. Cottages overlooking the Cricket Green, on what in Tom Francis's youth was still known as the Causeway. As far as one can tell, these houses were a little to the south of today's *Queen's Head*. In its section on Mitcham, the *Victoria County History* observed that, 'Many of the old cottages are entirely of timber construction, the quartering being externally covered with weather-boarding and the roofs tiled, while others are built partly of brick and partly of timber.' The appearance of these particular cottages on the Causeway is interesting, and the jettied upper floors suggest they might have been somewhat older than their sliding sash windows and plastered fronts would at first sight imply.

102. Some more old cottages, this time off Cranmer Road, near Cranmer Farm. The pantiled roofing was typical of many of the humbler dwellings still surviving in Mitcham towards the end of the 19th century. These cottages were demolished to provide a site for premises used as the Public Assistance Office during the inter-war period.

103. Another very small cottage, probably with its origins in a squatter's hovel, on Commonside West. No longer occupied as a dwelling in the 1880s, Tom Francis recalled that it was used for storage by Gardiner, the furniture dealer.

104. Although included in the Tom Francis collection, the photograph of these cottages in Love Lane, overlooking the West Fields, does not receive a mention in his lecture notes. Two rooms up and two down, and with single-storey back addition sculleries, these cottages were sturdily built in stock brick and with slate roofs. They probably dated to the 1830s, and the style was once fairly common in Mitcham. Only a handful now survive.

Farmhouses, Physic and Flower Gardens

In his description of Mitcham in 1884, Edward Walford commented that

> The soil of the parish is principally a rich black mould, and for upwards of a century a large proportion of the land hereabout has been cultivated for the production of sweet herbs and medicinal plants. Poppies, mint, liquorice, aniseed and chamomile have long been extensively grown here. Mitcham, it may be stated, is remarkable for the extent to which roses and other flowers are cultivated, and in fact, the parish has long been celebrated for its 'flower farms'. In summertime the air is perfumed by whole field of roses, lavender, and sweet and pleasant herbs; and probably there is not in all the kingdom a single parish on which the wholesale druggists and distillers of the metropolis draw more largely for their supplies ...

Several herbal distilleries were operating in Mitcham and just over the border in Carshalton and Croydon, extracting the essences not only from lavender, but also from peppermint, roses and sometime cedar. 'The essential oil was a valuable product', Tom recalled,

> the various herbs yielding but a small amount. When growers took their products to the distiller the receptacle for the oil was locked and the grower held the key. George Pitt at one time bought a derelict field of peppermint on which later he built Cyprus Terrace: he put his building staff to clearing the weeds and harvested his peppermint. It was a big surprise to him when the resulting essential oil was handed to him in a glass phial of small size.

105.   Pound Farm was probably one of the oldest buildings standing in the village during Tom Francis's early childhood. It occupied a site in London Road close by an old bridleway, which still survives as a public footpath, and once led towards the east common field of the medieval village. The farm derived its name from the pound of the manor of Biggin and Tamworth, which stood close by. 'Many farms of this type and age were in Mitcham', Tom Francis wrote in his notes. '"Gorringe", "Manor", "Church", "Rumbolt" and "Tamworth" and others now all gone.' Much of the land in East Fields formerly worked from Pound Farm was acquired in the 1880s by the Mizen brothers, Edward and Walter, market gardeners, who demolished the old farmhouse to provide a site for the erection of one of their greenhouses.

The situation was changing rapidly in Thomas Francis's youth, however, and Mitcham's physic gardens were soon to become history, giving way to nurseries and market gardens. Alfred Mizen, one of the three sons of the Edward Mizen who founded the market gardening firm of Mizen Brothers at Eastfields, Mitcham, was an old friend of Tom Francis. At its peak the firm had fields under cultivation off Western Road as well as towards Pollards Hill, and extensive greenhouses in the vicinity of Grove Road and Tamworth Lane.

Besides vegetables [Mizens produced] acres of flowers: roses, daffodils, narcissi, cloves, pinks, asters, cornflowers, sweet peas, chrysanthemum. Fields of these were a beautiful sight. As factories developed in the area and the air became heavily smoke laden quantities of gay coloured flowers and especially white flowers might be spoiled in a night if the wind blew in a certain direction. For this reason and others, our horticulturalists sought farms further afield, so Alfred Mizen told me

said Tom: 'Their firm opened up at Cobham and Leatherhead. Mitcham farm lands were disposed of for building and for sports grounds.'

106. The photograph of another old farmhouse, this time in the vicinity of the *Goat* public house, appears in the Tom Francis collection, but is unfortunately too indistinct to enable one to assess the building's age. Known in Tom's time as Rumbolt Farm, it was alleged that Archbishop Cranmer, who had been martyred at the stake in Oxford in 1556, had once lived there, but careful research into his family's history in the 18th century by James Cranmer, a lawyer by profession, failed to produce anything to support the tradition. As Henman's Farm, Rumbolts is first mentioned in a deed recording the purchase by Robert Cranmer of lands in Mitcham in about 1652, and what could well already have been an old house was subsequently 'modernised' by his son John c.1680. Some two hundred years later 'Rumbolds Farm' (as it was marked on Ordnance Survey maps) was demolished.

107. Tom Francis had no actual photographs of herb gardens or Mitcham field workers in his collection, and instead used this copy of a newspaper woodcut showing an artist's impression of the lavender harvest in Mitcham. He was uncertain of the date of the drawing, but guessed that it might have been around 1860, and understood that it was made in the region of Lavender Avenue, looking towards the cottages and farm buildings facing Figges Marsh. It was here, at Tamworth Farm, just to the north of the *Swan*, that Potter and Moore had their distillery for producing the essence for which Mitcham had been famous since the extraction of oil of lavender on a commercial scale had been started by Ephraim Potter and William Moore in 1749. Of the many known varieties of lavender, that grown in Mitcham was considered the most fragrant. The actual process of extracting the oil was quite simple, the bundles of freshly cut lavender being taken to the stills with the minimum delay, and there boiled in water. The vapour driven off passed through condensers and the distillate was then allowed to separate, the essential oil rising to the surface of the containers whilst the water remained at the bottom. According to Tom Francis's information, the lavender plants came to perfection in three years, when the best crop was gathered, but the bushes could be cropped for six years in succession before they were grubbed up. Relays of young bushes were planted yearly to provide replacements. The spent bushes were used to thatch the sides and ends of sheds, and many were stored away to help the annual blaze on 5 November.

108. Workers gathering the lavender harvest early one morning at Carshalton, probably on the Barrow Hedges estate. This picture, taken for R. M. Jones in about 1905 and published in the press, serves to remind one that after large scale commercial cultivation of lavender in Mitcham had ceased, the growing of medicinal and aromatic herbs continued in the parishes to the south until the early years of the 20th century. The harvesters used a small bagging hook, known as a 'mint hook'. Tom Francis sold dozens of them at London House, receiving orders from various parts of the country long after the Mitcham farms had vanished under suburban housing. He was once asked to send a supply to Tasmania. 'Members of the old Mitcham family of Slaters migrated to Australia, founded Mitcham, and grew lavender and were responsible for the commercialisation of Eucalyptus', he recorded in his lecture notes, and for some years before his death he was in correspondence with the authorities at one of the three Mitchams in Australia, 'exchanging courtesies' and supplying photographs of the fair to be included in the town's official guide.

109. Mr. Fowler, one of the last of the old Mitcham lavender growers. According to Tom Francis, after Fowler had given up actually growing the plant, he continued to trade in lavender. Although the physic gardens had gone, several distilleries remained in production in Mitcham (the last, W. J. Bush and Company, until the middle of the 20th century), drawing their supplies initially from elsewhere in Surrey and Norfolk, but eventually from France and Holland.

Old Inns and Public Houses

Mitcham in Tom Francis's day was well, if not over, provided with inns, public houses and beer houses. The main cause, in his opinion, was 'probably the big number of persons employed in Mitcham in the many busy works', but 'the village position on one of the south coast roads and the many coaches and other travellers passing through' were also factors.

The Francis family were staunch teetotallers, and perhaps for this reason the Tom Francis collection of slides and photographs is not so rich in illustrations of Mitcham's hostelries as it might otherwise have been. Many of the inns which survived until the end of the 19th century were of great age, and their structures provided an interesting record of the changes which had taken place in vernacular architecture and building techniques over perhaps three hundred years.

110.   The Tom Francis collection of slides does not contain a good photograph of what is probably Mitcham's best known public house, the former *King's Head* at the corner of the Cricket Green and London Road. This photograph, taken from outside the *White Hart* in about 1870 is, however, interesting, not only for what one can glimpse of the side of the *King's Head* and its outbuildings, but also for what one can see of the unmade road outside and the chickens, which could then wander about safely. The projecting single-storey pantiled building was a smithy. 'Leech, the barber, operated here about 1880', noted Tom. The rear part of the inn, in which there is a fine panelled room, dates at least to the early 17th century, whilst the more imposing front portion, not shown in this photograph, is of about 1760, and was almost certainly erected to provide better facilities with which to attract the custom of passengers on the stagecoaches. In pre-motoring days the *King's Head* was very busy during the Epsom races, and it was here that the coach of the future Edward VII, when Prince of Wales, used to stop whilst the horses were changed. It was also at the *King's Head*, so local legend had it, that the Prince was insulted by the assembled crowd, and thereafter made the journey to Epsom by train. Until the 1890s an old pollarded elm by the roadside outside the inn was adorned with a crudely carved and coloured head of a king. 'It was anything but a work of art', observed Tom, 'and we were not depressed when we found the king's head crowned by an upturned pail of coal tar. The tar ran in thick streams down the monarch's face, and he was removed. Later the tree was cut down.'

111.   The *Surrey Arms* in Morden Road, photographed before it was demolished and a new mock-Tudor public house erected in its place in the 1930s. The old pub, the adjacent cottage and the tall white house, the latter known variously as the White House, White Cottage, or Casablanca, formed an attractive grouping of typical Surrey weatherboarded buildings. Sadly, only the White House now survives. An artesian well had been sunk at the back of the house by Robert Ellis, a local mineral water manufacturer, and there was an iron drinking fountain at the roadside, complete with chained metal cup and an inscription. Ellis's son sank a similar deep well in Western Road, where he opened a mineral water bottling factory (the Ravenspring Works) in 1877. Workmen engaged in sinking the well used to report finding shells deep in the boring, but it was rumoured that these finds were fictitious, and simply made for the beer money the 'Gov'nor' gave for them. (In actual fact, fossil shells would not have been all that remarkable, since the bore reached a depth of 233 ft. below ground level, penetrating 16 ft. through a stratum of chalk-with-flints, and a further 84 ft. into the chalk.) Tom concluded his note on the slide with the comments that the 'C.A.M.W.A.L. people (the Chemists' Aerated Mineral Water Company Ltd.) took the works over after Ellis', and that the name of the *Fountain* public house on the other side of Western Road had been inspired by the artesian well opposite.

112.   The *Three Kings* public house on Commonside East, photographed in 1869. The old building, with its 18th-century brick façade, was pulled down and replaced by the present mock-Tudor building in 1928.

113. The *Ravensbury Arms* on the Croydon Road, in the centre of Mitcham Common, photographed in 1869. Named after the manor of Ravensbury (the manor pound for straying cattle stood close by) the pub was also known as the *Blue House*. From here to the *Gardeners' Arms*, or *Red House*, on the Croydon boundary was about a mile, and the road between the two was a favourite course for trotting and pony races. The old timber-framed and weatherboarded *Ravensbury Arms* was demolished when the present inn was built in 1906.

114. The *Swan* inn, London Road, photographed in 1870. With its water trough in front, this was a favourite stopping place for the covered wagons of the carriers, and was a good example of an unpretentious, workaday village inn. The steps leading up to the front door enabled cellarage to be provided without excavating below the level of the ground water which here, as in much of Mitcham, was only a few feet below the surface.

115.   The High Street, Upper Mitcham, in 1865, looking north from the Fair Green. The old *Buck's Head* is on the right, and
a weatherboarded *King's Arms* appears on the left. Beyond, one can glimpse the gable end of a draper's shop kept by Lack.
This building seems to have been of jettied construction, which suggests it could have been some three hundred years old. All
were demolished shortly after 1900, when the road was widened a few feet, but it still remained an awkward bottleneck for
traffic.

The Common

Walford described 'the broad expanse of Mitcham Common' in 1884 as an 'open breezy spot ... for the most part bare and bleak' and quoted Weale for whom it was 'an immense but not very pleasing tract, being so completely unplanted, and having so very few villas on its margins'. This was no exaggeration, since for centuries the Common had been used and abused by local people gathering timber and brushwood for fuel and over-grazing with cattle, sheep and horses, which prevented regeneration of the trees and bushes. More seriously, indiscriminate gravel digging was becoming widespread, and by the 1870s and '80s the Common was degenerating into what another writer described as a treeless waste of 'whin, swamp and gravel pits'. It was, moreover, under constant threat from the railway companies and others who, by illicit enclosure, sought to profit from what they often argued was the 'betterment' of derelict land. At that time few had the vision to forsee the need to conserve the Common as open space for recreation, or could appreciate its potential ecological interest. Fortunately, several influential local residents, led by George Parker Bidder Q.C., of Ravensbury Park, were active in securing the passage of the necessary legislation through Parliament to bring the Common within the provisions of the Metropolitan Commons Acts of 1866 and 1869. Following the enactment of the necessary legislation, a Board of Common Conservators was formed in 1891 and byelaws were soon in force regulating future use of the Common. Tragically, Bidder was not destined to witness the full success of his efforts for he was killed in a street accident in 1896. A granite monument to his memory, erected by public subscription near the centre of the Common, can still be seen between the Seven Islands pond and the Croydon Road.

With the acquisition of mineral rights from the lords of the manors in 1894 the Conservators were soon able to bring the practice of gravel digging to an end. A further achievement was the final abolition of the ancient practice of grazing animals on common land. After a hearing lasting four days at Croydon the Conservators were successful in obtaining an injunction against Henry ('Jaeger') Bankes, prohibiting him from turning out cattle on the Common. The matter was not finally settled until 1909, however, when a High Court ruling was given in favour of the Conservators, and thereafter grazing ended.

Much of the Common had by this time become devoted to golfing, the Conservators having granted the exclusive Princes Golf Club a lease of land in 1891 for the construction of an 18-hole course and the erection of a clubhouse. Although not barred from access to the Common, many people came to the conclusion that the scarlet-coated golfers were monopolising what local residents had begun to regard and appreciate as public open space. Eventually, as a result of popular pressure and much bad feeling, the course was restricted to only half the Common.

A major enclosure of common land, sanctioned in the late 18th century for the erection of a parish workhouse, could be seen as having been in the public interest.

A century later, no longer needed for its original purpose, the old workhouse had been incorporated into the Woodite Works (Pl.123). The red-brick building with its prominent clock was erected by Mitcham vestry in 1782 to house the poor and destitute of the parish. It ceased to be used as a workhouse in 1838 when, following reform of the administration of the poor law, Mitcham was joined with other localities to form the Croydon Union and accommodation became available in the new workhouse at Duppas Hill, Croydon. In 1857, after pressure from several local residents an attempt was made by the vestry to secure demolition of the building and return of the land to the Common, from which the three acres had been enclosed with consent of the lord of the Mitcham manor of Biggin and Tamworth. James Bridger, who had inherited the lordship of the manor, opposed the proposition, arguing that, since one of his predecessors had sanctioned the use of the land and the erection of the building, the structure was his, and he intended to dispose of it as a factory. The premises have remained in industrial use ever since, but for a century or more after their vacation by the Guardians of the Poor, the path across the Common leading from *Blue House* bridge to the former workhouse continued to be known as the 'Workhouse Path'.

Tom Francis used to intrigue audiences at his lantern slide talks with various grisly stories of the old workhouse, probably recounting tales he had heard from his father, including the alleged activities of body snatchers. 'These gentry,' he said, 'worked for a retaining fee (£50) and so much per body (£9), their clients being doctors and students [who required them] for anatomical purposes. It is also said', he assured his listeners, 'that in spite of the loss of corpses the funerals had to take place from the workhouse as though nothing wrong had happened.'

After it had been sold the workhouse was used as a lucifer match factory,

stoutish wood sticks with phosphorus tops, a big advance on flint and tinder. Later the building was taken over by a rubber factory. Buildings were added and from here ground sheets and waterproof clothing was sent for soldiers in the Crimea [in] 1856. Hoopers the Cable Makers here [*sic*] assembled – made Submarine Cable for Persian Gulf, Pacific and North Sea but not, I think, as some declare, the great Atlantic Cable. Hooper gave up the works and later the Woodite Works were established. Woodite was an elastic composition for coating ships and tyres and such smaller things as golf balls. It was rumoured that a mechanical horse was produced to go before the new horseless carriages. It did not appear on the roads. Mrs. Woods built a castle of flint for her home and also a chapel in the grounds ... The workers wore white blouses similar in shape to the battle jacket of today. London House stocked them and when the works were closed down ... they were then unsaleable.

116. The *Three Kings* pond, photographed in October *c*.1900, looking along Commonside West. Unfortunately this was taken before the days of colour film, and it was to Tom Francis's regret that he was unable to capture the full beauty of the early morning mist and the autumn foliage. The boundary wall of the Elmwood estate can be seen on the right. Here, utilising the road frontage, Isaac Wilson was to build the row of shops which became the property of the Wilson Hospital Trust. The pond takes the water from what had once been an open ditch running along the side of Commonside East, and overflows through a culvert passing underneath Commonside West. Shortly before the First World War the pond was cleaned out, cemented, and for safety railed where the road passed alongside. Tom Francis remembered the pond as 'a great place for sliding and skating in winter', and a time when during particularly harsh and prolonged frost the ice became thick enough for 'an eccentric old fellow living at Verandah Cottage to drive his waggonette across'.

117. A somewhat indifferent photograph, but of historical interest in that it shows the *Three Kings* Piece and Commonside East shortly before 1866 when the London, Brighton and South Coast Railway Company constructed its branch line from Streatham to Mitcham Junction. In 1877 a proposal for a new line which, by avoiding the curve taken by the original branch, would allow trains to cross the Common without slackening speed, was abandoned in the face of strong opposition from local residents, who objected to the loss of yet more common land.

118. Mitcham Junction station on Mitcham Common, a photograph produced from a wet-plate negative taken probably not long after the station had been opened by the London Brighton and South Coast Railway Company in 1868. The arrival of a train was still treated as an important event, to be acknowledged by the presence on the platform of the station master, resplendent in top hat and morning coat. Between Wimbledon and Mitcham Junction stations the line (opened in 1855) was single track, and a metal baton had to be surrendered to the station staff by the train crew before the 'clear' signal could be given and the train proceed on its journey. Tom Francis, like all small boys, was fascinated by the engine used on the Wimbledon to Croydon line through Mitcham. He thought it to be 'all that an engine should be. It was a standard [of] beauty and efficiency for all locomotives. In comparison the more powerful engines on the main lines were ugly. In spite of this, or because of it, our beautiful little engine was called *The Old Tea Kettle*.'

119. *Three Kings* Piece in about 1895,
looking towards Commonside East.
Hancock's Cottages, the *Three Kings* and
an 18th-century red-brick house which
stood next door can be glimpsed through
the trees. Lombardy poplars were then
somewhat more of a feature of the
Mitcham landscape than at the present
time and, although not an indigenous
species, several groups had been planted
as quick-growing screens, notably by men
like Isaac Wilson and Harry Mallaby-
Deeley, who occupied The Birches and
Mitcham Court, overlooking the Cricket
Green.

120. John H. Francis paddling a canoe
on the Seven Islands pond. This pond, in
the centre of the Common, dates from
about 1900, when excavations left by
gravel diggers, often deep pools and
hillocks, were levelled and trimmed into
shape. In one part the Seven Islands pond
was deepened and marked with boundary
posts so that it could be used as a
swimming pool. This was an early
attempt by Mitcham to encourage
swimming. A small hut was erected for
the schools, and in summer the pool
became very popular. The pond was
occasionally also used for sailing, and it
was a favourite with model boat
enthusiasts.

121.   For many small boys one of the great fascinations of the Common was the large number of small ponds, a legacy of the gravel diggers, in which frogs, newts, sticklebacks, snails, leeches and many queer water insects could be caught in a net or with a worm on a bent pin. Fishing for 'tiddlers' proved an almost irresistible attraction.

122.   A gorse fire on the Common. Gorse and wild broom flourished on the Common in the 1880s, and fires occurred frequently in the summer when the bushes were dry. Sometimes efforts were made by the fire brigade to extinguish the flames, but left to themselves the fires usually burnt out. The bushes soon grew again, although after a bad fire full recovery might take several years. 'Considerable tracts of gorse were destroyed intentionally to make the fairways for the Princes Golf Club course. When people did pretty much as they wished about the Common, local bakers cut the furze for heating their bread ovens. Fires were lit in the oven until it was heated sufficiently, the embers were withdrawn and the bread baked.' Quantities of furze were also chopped away and dragged home for bonfires on 5 November. On occasions of national celebration, such as Coronations, Royal weddings and Jubilees, huge fires were built on the Common for everyone's enjoyment.

123. The red-brick building of Mitcham's 18th-century workhouse can be seen here over the wall of the Woodite works. Before being destroyed by blast in 1941 the building had been used at different times for producing motors, margarine, raising mushrooms and as a warehouse for paints and fertilisers.

124. Mrs. Woods' house, The Towers and its chapel, both of which had been erected in the style of mock-gothic follies, were destroyed by blast from a parachute mine dropped on the Common during an air raid in 1941. At the same time the old workhouse building of 1782 sustained severe damage. The sites were redeveloped for industrial purposes within a short time of the rubble being cleared away.

125. The windmill on Mitcham Common, photographed in 1900. The sails and outbuildings are reflected in a nearby pool formed in a disused gravel pit. The mill was a hollow post mill, the whole of the upper part of the structure capable of being turned by hand to face into the wind. It had been erected in 1806, following a grant of enclosure by James Moore, lord of the manor of Biggin and Tamworth, given on the condition that on two days a week the miller should grind the grist of the inhabitants of Mitcham at a 'fair price'. According to Tom Francis, the mill was working until 1860, and remained a picturesque feature on the Common for a number of years, attracting the attention of artists like W. Sleath and George Haité, who in later life became president of the Society of English Decorators. As a boy, Haité painted local scenes for pocket money. The old mill was struck by a 'ball of fire' and severely damaged during a thunderstorm in 1878, but two sails remained until the upper part of the mill was dismantled in about 1906, leaving only the circular base, with its conical roof. The original miller's house stood by the mill, and was replaced in the latter half of the 19th century by the present, larger, Mill House. Tom commented that the land which finally came to be enclosed by the garden fence was considerably more extensive than that originally sanctioned.

126. Tom Francis describes this avenue of trees, which would appear to be mainly oak, as leading 'from the footbridge over the London, Brighton and South Coast railway towards Beddington Lane by the boundary of the original golf course for ladies. The Club House,' he says, 'was built on the angle of land made by the two railway lines. It was reached from Princes Course by a wood footbridge. Women later played on the main course with the men.' Both courses had been established and the club houses erected before publication of the revised Ordnance Survey maps of 1894. A number of the trees, or their seedlings, still survive today, marking the southern margin of Mitcham Common. Beyond this lies the 'Hundred Acres', a tract of former common land within the parish of Mitcham enclosed and added to the Beddington estate under the authority of an act of Parliament passed in 1819.

127.   The *Ravensbury Arms* and the *Blue House* cottages, probably photographed in the late 1860s. The Ravensbury manor pound stood behind the cottages, which appear to have been erected around 1781. The cottages were held on copyhold tenure of the manor of Ravensbury, and are shown as an 'encroachment' in maps produced in the early 19th century.

128.   A group of willow trees, described by Tom Francis in his notes as being on Commonside East. Tom attributed their origin to having been 'planted, as many were on the common, as posts for clothes lines for hanging out the washing. Such groups of three or four or more willow posts which had taken root could be seen on other parts of the common near the Causeway, by Cranmer Farm, on the Green near the Methodist Chapel and near the National Schools. They were kept short as pollards and most eventually blew down.'

Mitcham Cricket and the Lower Green

Lower Mitcham Green lay within the manor of Vauxhall, and had been part of the extensive common pasture or 'waste' of the medieval parish. For centuries it had provided grazing for those who could claim the right by virtue of their tenure of properties 'held of the manor'. It undoubtedly survived the enclosure movement of the late 18th and early 19th centuries largely because it was recognised, in the words of one surveyor reporting in 1806, as 'the best feature of the village ... on which there is much Cricket playing'. He strongly advised the Dean and Chapter of Canterbury, who then held the lordship of the manor, against any attempt to sell off part of the Green for housing, as this would provoke an adverse reaction from local people.

It would now appear that organised cricket had been played on the Green for some three hundred years, and whereas by Tom Francis's time for a century or more the Mitcham Cricket Club had assumed prescriptive rights over the eastern half of the Lower Green the 'Cricket Green' proper – this had not always gone unchallenged. Mitcham public have always defended what they considered 'their rights' and as late as the 19th century cattle, sheep and horses were turned out on the Green, and geese and chickens treated it as their own. Grazing was brought to an end by the Mitcham Common Conservators, in whom the Green was vested, along with the other common lands, in 1891. According to Tom Francis, a Green Preservation Society was formed at one time to conserve the Green as an amenity, and attempted to assert rights which it did not possess. They were perhaps before their time and, unable to sustain support, the society seems to have collapsed. Passions could be aroused when the Green was under threat, however, and when an attempt was made by the local authority in the 1930s to widen London Road it was frustrated by general opposition to any 'improvements' which were at the expense of the Green itself.

If parts of the Lower Green were regarded without question as public property, this did not extend to the hallowed cricket field, and Tom Francis recalled in his notes the case of one individual who was so misguided as to gallop a horse across the Green and the cricket pitch. He was taken before the court at Croydon and convicted. Two of the many footpaths which once cut across the Green still survive, but since 1905 the public has been kept from the cricket field itself by rails, the old hurdles of Tom's boyhood days no longer providing adequate protection as the population of Mitcham began to increase.

At one time Mitcham Rugby Club used the Green regularly on Saturdays and Boxing Day, but they caused considerable damage to the cricket pitch, and were persuaded to shift their ground to Commonside West. For a short time tennis was played on the triangle of Green opposite Elm Court (now Mitcham Court) by people living in the big house. Hockey was also played for a while in winter on the part of the Green opposite the police station.

In his reminiscences of the closing years of the Victorian period, Tom Francis recollected that in the 1890s Mitcham Cricket Club did not play at home on Bank

Holidays, which gave a chance for the occasional cricketers amongst the shopkeepers and tradesmen, Upper and Lower Mitcham, and the Young Men's Club, to enjoy themselves. Also at this time,

> there were fewer Mitcham Cricket Club matches in the centre than now, but often three games were in progress at once. Mitcham on the centre, The Wanderers parallel to the footpath [from the] Vestry Hall to Cold Blows, [and] The Old Buffer's opposite the *Britannia*. (The old pub was their headquarters) One of the extraordinary games recorded is the match between 'The Early Risers' and 'The Peep O' Day Boys' consisting of Mitcham men who in those days had little time for sport – shops were open from 8 a.m. to 9 p.m., Saturdays 11-12 p.m. Stumps were pitched at 3.30 a.m. Coffee was supplied by an enterprising stall holder. My Uncle Bill played and my father was an umpire. I think the 'Old Buffer' (Fred Gale) sponsored the game.

The Green in general on Bank Holidays and summer evenings had more games in progress than one would see now. 'In the evenings the lads and lasses played "rounders", "leap-frog" and "Kiss in the Ring". Very popular if judged by the size of the ring,' Tom remembered with amusement.

129.   Mitcham Cricket Green in 1900, with a match in progress. At this time still very much a typical village green, it was surrounded by tall trees and had no railings. There was also no pavilion, so tents were erected for visitors and the players. The scorer for Mitcham sometimes scored from a tent, and for a long period the balcony of the *Cricketers* was used. Later a special wooden hut was wheeled out and then, in 1904, came the present pavilion on the Causeway behind the *King's Head*.

CRICKET.

A Grand Match

Will be Played

At Lower Mitcham Green,

On Monday, July 30th, and following Day,

BETWEEN

Eleven Gentlemen of the Parish of Mitcham, against Eleven Gentlemen of the Parish of Godalmin, for

100 Guineas a Side.

The Wickets to be pitched at 10 o'Clock precisely.

PLAYERS.

MITCHAM.	GODALMIN.
W. C. Dyer, Esq.	Weller Ladbroke, Esq.
Chesteman,	Lambert, Esq.
Sherman,	Keene, Esq.
James Sherman,	Hull,
Bowyer,	Grinham,
Bailey,	James Grinham,
Chilman,	Marshall,
Haile,	Smith,
Asprey,	Flavell,
Shepherd,	Searle,
Rutter,	Peto,
Tiptaft,	Methurst,
Merritt,	Homer,

A Good Ordinary at the King's Head, at 2 o'Clock each day.

130. A poster of c.1840, advertising a cricket match at Mitcham between 11 gentlemen of Mitcham and 11 from Godalming 'for 100 Guineas a Side'. The names of the Mitcham players were familiar to Tom Francis from the days of his youth, and included several whose reputation extended beyond their native Green. The two Shermans, father and son, Bowyer, Bailey, Haile, Asprey, Shepherd and Rutter – all were idolised by young Tom and his contemporaries, born in a village which had been renowned for its Green and its cricketers since the early years of the 18th century, when the men of Mitcham could throw down the cricketing gauntlet to London. In one such match, reported in the *County Journal* of 26 June 1730, Mitcham won 'by a considerable number of notches', and by 1736 was considered to have one of the best greens in Surrey. The club's pre-eminence was certainly not diminished by the passage of time, for when Surrey played England at Lords in 1810 no less than five of the players on the county side were Mitcham men, and in 1813 the village was strong enough to play the Marylebone Club in a two-day match on their home ground. Three years later Mitcham's reputation must have taken a serious knock, for in a match against Gravesend in 1816 they were beaten by 10 wickets and 2 runs, scoring 19 and 17 against Gravesend's 38! Another notice belonging to Mitcham Cricket Club which Tom Francis had seen advertised a match for money against Dorking in 1844, and prompted the recollection that 'sporting games' had once been common in 'the bad old days of cricket', and were often organised by 'noblemen' for big stakes. Stories were told of betting taking place freely on the grounds, and of games being so dominated on occasions by money makers' 'legs' that both sides might have been offered and taken bribes to lose, and winning became a farce. 'Cricket had become anything but "cricket"', said Tom, but 'the purge at last came and thoroughly "cleaned up" the game.'

131. An old time cricketer, believed by Tom Francis to have been Tom Sherman's father, one of Mitcham's cricketing 'greats' of the early 19th century. He was happily captured for posterity in this faded ferrotype photograph, copied by Tom for his slide collection.

132. John Bowyer, another of Mitcham's grand old men of cricket, in a cartoon by Collingsby, drawn in 1879 when John was about 89 years of age. Bowyer lodged with the Misses Wasley (who were not pleased to see him depicted in petticoats) in one of the pair of weatherboarded cottages in Whitford Lane next to the London Store, and he was often to be found leaning over the garden gate smoking a long churchwarden pipe. He and Tom Francis, then aged seven, were great friends and exchanged confidences. Old John laid claim to more than a nodding acquaintance with Lord Nelson, who was in the practice of driving over from Merton Place to Mitcham Green with Lady Hamilton to watch the cricket. John's fondest memory of the great man was his last visit, shortly before departing on the journey which ended at Trafalgar, when he gave John a shilling 'to drink to the confusion of the French'. Bowyer was then a lad of 15, and already playing for Mitcham. Sir Cato Worsfold, of Hall Place, was another who took delight in encouraging old John to tell his stories, and there is no doubt that he could draw upon a rich store of memories, for he had played for Surrey and the South of England from 1810 to 1828. When past active cricket, he stood umpire for Mitcham for more than thirty years, and was rewarded with a benefit match for his service to the club. When John Bowyer died in 1880 at the age of 90, a bat was placed on his coffin and carried with him to the grave.

"GINX's BABY"

133. Cricketers on Lower Mitcham Green in 1869, when players were not so particular about their costume. The photograph was taken from the *White Hart* corner for Thomas Francis senior by Drummond, using the wet-plate process. The black-coated figure to the left is John Bowyer, who umpired the game, and the group seems also to have included James Southerton and the Humphries boys, Tom, William and Richard, all of whom played for Mitcham between 1862 and 1874.

134. James Southerton, landlord of the *Cricketers* at Mitcham, portrayed in another of Collingsby's cartoons, dated 1879. Southerton played for Surrey from 1854-55, and then for Sussex and Hampshire. He reappeared for Surrey as an effective bowler with a slow round arm action, taking four wickets for five runs in a match against the M.C.C. first team in 1872, when the London team was dismissed for 16! According to Tom Francis, Southerton walked to and from the Oval for his matches. He also remembered him as 'a friendly chap' who 'played a lot on the Green' and 'would bowl to us youngsters on his way out to the nets'. Southerton was accused by his friends of shutting his eyes when he batted, but he was deemed good enough to be selected twice to play for England in Australia! The cartoon had been drawn with a kangaroo body which, for the purpose of making the slide, Tom Francis altered to that of a cricketer. The caption read: 'Our James contrived a double game to play; Draughts at night and cricketing by day.' The original drawing was presented by Francis to Southerton's son-in-law, Athol Harwood who lived in the first of the two wooden cottages next to the Francis family's shop, when first married.

135. Tom Richardson, born 1870, learnt his cricket at Mitcham, where his parents moved when he was a boy. Tall and powerful, he became a great fast bowler much to the discomfort of W. G. Grace, according to Tom Francis. A member of the Wanderers and Mitcham XI, Richardson played for Surrey from 1892 until 1901, and for England against Australia. He was also a member of the 'The Old Buffers' club.

136. Herbert Strudwick, another Mitcham boy, born 1880, who became a great wicket-keeper. A member of the Wanderers and Mitcham XI like Richardson, he played for Surrey in 1900 and for England against Australia both at home and 'down under'.

137. The end of an innings, c.1900. A batsman retires pensively from the field, watched by a future generation of cricketers. A row of posts and rails can be seen on the far side of the path leading to Cold Blows, but the Green is still open to the roadside. Until the Board of Conservators took over responsibility, the Green, the cricket pitch and the outfield were the concern of Mitcham Cricket Club, supported liberally by wealthy patrons. One such was Charles H. Hoare of The Canons, treasurer of Surrey for a number of years, who played for the county from 1846-53. 'Under his keen support Mitcham Cricket was alive', said Tom Francis. 'Fred Gale was a worthy successor to Hoare and encouraged youthful players. He it was who had the green bush drained.' This was successful for a number of years, but in the end a better system became necessary, and through the efforts of W. W. Thompson, backed by the Surrey County Club with £25, being half the cost, the Green was pipe drained. 'It is something to their credit that the Green ... is still green with vigorous turf after 200 years or more of cricket, football, hockey, quoits, grazing horses and children's play, not to mention athletic sports, leap frog, rounders, kiss-in-the-ring, various celebrations, swings and cokernut [sic] shies ...', mused Tom in 1946.

Mitcham Fair and Fairgoers

Old Mitcham Fair featured prominently in Tom Francis's memories and, once he had equipped himself with a camera, both fair and fairgoers provided almost limitless opportunities for capturing scenes and faces which otherwise would have passed unrecorded. Although claimed by some of its supporters to be a Charter Fair, Mitcham Fair is in reality merely a customary fair, held until the early years of this century with the consent of the lord of the manor of Biggin and Tamworth, who derived an income from the tolls collected by his steward. As Tom put it, 'the Council, or Vestry in those days, had no finger in the pie, and the letting of plots was arranged by an agent of the lord of the manor'. The fair lasted for three days, from 12-14 August, but caravans were allowed to draw on to the fair ground on the eleventh. Opening was at 12 o'clock on the 12th, unless that day fell on a Sunday, in which case the fair did not start until the following Monday. All caravans were required to move off the Green on the day after the fair closed.

Some romantics declared that there was a tradition that horses had to be sold at the commencement of the fair, but although undoubtedly some animals changed hands at fair time, there is nothing to show that opening was conditional on sales actually taking place. 'In my early days,' declared Tom, 'there was little or no ceremony: at 12 noon the organ of the roundabout let go, the whistle blew and that was that. In the *Nag's Head* pub could be seen on the wall of the bar a modest sized key with the inscription below 'Key of the Fair'.' It does not seem, from his remarks, that in those days the key played any significant part in the opening.

Swings large and small were part of the earliest fairs Tom Francis could remember, and there was a version of the big wheel, called the 'Highover', which had four swinging boats. 'Early roundabouts were sent twirling by gear worked by the proprietor with a handle', said Tom. 'Larger ones were set going by the owner assisted by boys, who pushed the cars and horses round till a good speed was worked up. They then jumped on themselves. Later roundabouts were run on steam though often the music was supplied by hand.'

In Tom's father's boyhood days there were several large tents devoted to dancing, but it would seem these were no longer a feature of the fair by the 1880s, for they are not described in the lecture notes. Dioramas were popular, as were marionettes and peep shows. There were also many side shows more reminiscent of the circus, including performing dogs and monkeys, sword throwers, jugglers and acrobats. 'Monstrosities were always on show. Fat women, living skeletons, dwarfs and fat boys turned up nearly every year.' The advertising pictures hung in front of the tents 'were colourful and coarse and very extravagant announcements and portrayals of wonders to be seen for two or three pence. The lettering was gaily coloured and of the type reserved for Fairs and Showmen's announcements'. Tom also recalled that

Mitcham lads were always interested in the boxing shows where in the glare of Naptha lamps the fighting men would be introduced by the Proprietor advertising their prowess and their willingness to 'take on' anybody in the crowd. Gloves were thrown to the acceptors (often members of the boxing team distributed in the crowd). Wonderful pictures of famous fighters decorated the outside of the tents. Fighting and wrestling females were also an attraction.

The goods on sale at the Fair were of no great value, nothing much costing more than 1/-, principally dolls, toys, drums, trumpets, wonderful silvered glass vases, china ornaments and such, and common jewellery ... A vendor was generally found offering 'gold' rings which he placed in a coloured paper packet accompanied by a halfcrown – the whole lot for 3d. The halfcrowns, however, never left their owner.

Travelling salesmen and cheapjacks without allotted pitches on the Fair Ground were often present. One such, a purveyor of very crude rag dolls, did a roaring trade from his wagonette, lit by a flaring lamp. His description of his goods, the dolls, as 'the only legitimate toy in the Fair for a female child' was certainly original.

Stallholders at the fair had probably always dealt in 'toys and fairings', and trading in items under these general headings continued well into the 20th century. Itinerant hawkers were common in Mitcham during Tom Francis's boyhood and, if their wares were somewhat suspect, they could claim toleration on account of the entertainment they obviously provided. Tom tells us that they

often set up quite elaborate stages in public house yards (*White Hart* for instance) and by Baby Shows and Competitions attracted crowds and many customers. The Salesman's methods too were startling, for occasionally, to the gasps of the crowds, if he failed to get a responsive bid for his wares, he would smash the lot with his hammer! As to 'quacks' ... Pills and Potions were their stock in trade and their oratory, their persuasiveness and their knowledge of common ills that flesh is heir to induced the nimble 6d. or 1s. to leave the pockets of the crowd for their own. 'Corn cure' was a popular article of commerce.

Coloured paper shavings tied to a stick to flick in people's faces and sometimes peacock feathers for tickling helped to make the 'fun of the fair'.

Tom also mentions 'Tormentors', which he describes as 'metal tubes filled with water', sold for 2d. or 3d. each.

The caps unscrewed and you were free to squirt all and sundry. These were considered 'great fun' by the purchasers, but were frowned upon by the 'Authorities'. Police notices were posted prohibiting their use, but the notices were little heeded until action followed and quite respectable lads were marched through Cold Blows to the Police Station; were let out on bail and had to appear at Croydon Court and pay up the fine. This finally put a damper on the 'Tormentor' market.

Shooting Galleries were very popular. In some you shot at a target down long tubes [and] a 'bull' made the bell ring. Another type (for good shots) were light balls or eggshells supported by jets of steam or water, the balls always on the move up or down. However, the most satisfactory range was where glass bottles were suspended on wires, dozens of them. They were 'sitting targets' but it was very satisfactory to bring 'em down. The crash of glass gave us our money's value! This type of shooting range was later considered dangerous to the public and the police suppressed firing at suspended bottles.

For many years it had been obvious that the local police force was quite inadequate to deal with the riff-raff which the fair attracted, and strong reinforcements were supplied from neighbouring localities to patrol the ground. According to Tom Francis, the chief misdemeanour with which they had to contend, however, was pocket picking. Generally speaking a blind eye was turned on gambling games, it being difficult to draw a very clear line between skill and chance.

With consumer protection legislation in its infancy little, if any, thought was given to controlling the ingredients used in the foods offered at the fair, or to hygienic handling. 'Let the buyer beware' must have been the maxim. Tom remembered

> the 'eats' to be bought were whelks and cockles, gingerbreads and some you bought for your friends, hot with cayenne pepper! [There was] Ice cream, of course, and cokernuts [*sic*]. Then there was striped rock, dark and light shades of brown. This was manufactured on the fair ground in the morning. If you saw the process you decided to buy no more rock. After boiling a while in a plastic state it was pulled and thrown over a hook and pulled again and again ... and finally when it cooled was cut into the desired chunks. When it was hot the manufacturer spat on his hands to prevent it sticking!

Fair rock was often offered as a prize in games of chance. 'Chunks were arranged in a circle, like the figures of a clock, in the centre of which was a polished brass indicator on a pivot. For a modest halfpenny you could give it a twist, and when it stopped the rock, big or small, was yours. "A Ha'penny turn at the Rock, my dears and they're all good ha'porth."'

Control of Mitcham's Upper Green – the Fair Green – passed into the hands of the Board of Conservators of Mitcham Common in 1891, and in 1906 the Conservators purchased the franchise of the fair from the manor of Biggin and Tamworth. The physical extent of the fair was, of course, restricted by the Green itself, but various activities took place in adjoining yards and forecourts and, in later years, the fair tended to overflow into adjacent private land. Although regarded by middle class residents and many of the shopkeepers as an intolerable nuisance, attempts in the past to do away with the fair had failed. Matters were brought to a head once again by the extension of the London electric tramways from Tooting to Croydon in 1906. Increasing congestion at the Upper Green and the obvious danger from tramcars passing through the crowds attracted to the fair provided fresh justification for a renewed attempt by rural district and parish councillors, several of whom were also on the Board of Conservators, to secure suppression of the fair altogether.

The suggestion that the time had come for Mitcham Fair to be abolished provoked a strong reaction, not least from the Showmen's Guild. The fair was emotively dubbed 'the people's fair', much was made of its antiquity, and the claim was advanced that the fair had been established by a royal charter granted by Queen Elizabeth I. Despite searches, however, nothing was produced to substantiate the claim. Although it was becoming clear that eventually a solution would have to be found, such was the strength of the opposition to the proposal that the matter was shelved once again. It was not until the passing of the Mitcham Urban District Council Act in 1923, which vested control of the fair in the hands of the local authority, that it finally became possible to relocate the fair on the *Three Kings* Piece, where it is still held today.

138. Old Mitcham Fair: the opening ceremony, performed by a representative of the Showmen's Guild, probably a year or so before the outbreak of the First World War. The large golden key, which is still prominently displayed on opening day, made its first appearance at the time the fair was under threat in the early 1900s, and seems to have been produced by the showmen.

139.   Mitcham Fair in 1896, seen from the corner of Whitford Lane, with the old *Buck's Head* visible in the distance. At this time it was just a typical country fair and nothing to compare with the huge annual fair held since 1924 on the *Three Kings* Piece, between Commonside East and Commonside West.

140.   Crowd assembled on the Fair Green, probably at one of the protest meetings organised by the Showmen's Guild around 1906.

141. Another view of the fair, taken from the southern side of what came to be known as Upper Green West, looking towards Western Road. The apparent inversion of the print is an illusion; the lettering is seen from the reverse side of a painted canvas. By custom the big horse roundabout was always sited on this part of the Green.

142. Coconut shies were an ever-popular attraction at the fair. Here a local lad gives vent to what Tom Francis dubbed 'The Opening Bawl', to drum up interest. A certain class of Mitcham people were not noted for having quiet voices, and it appears their normal method of communication, a raucous bellow, was sarcastically referred to by inhabitants of neighbouring villages as a 'Mitcham Whisper'.

143.   Travellers' caravans on the Common during fair time. Mitcham Fair acted as a magnet for gypsies whether they were actually involved in running the fair or not. The caravans in the photograph, on which are hung baskets of various kinds and wicker chairs, are of interest. These travelling stores, which as well as basketry sold brooms and brushes, rugs and mats, used to be a fairly common sight, and their proprietors used to cry their wares around Mitcham streets.

144.   Mitcham Fair in 1896, looking south towards Whitford Lane, where the roofs of Thomas Francis's London Store can just be seen, rising above the awnings of the sideshows.

145. A view of the eastern side of the Fair Green, looking towards Samson's house, with the trees of Langdale Walk on the right. Tom Francis was referring to the contraption in the centre of this picture when he wrote: 'Local navvies were pleased to show their strength by hitting a wooden peg and sending up the indicator to make the bell ring at the top of a 20ft. board'.

146. A view of Mitcham Fair in about 1890, taken from James Drewett's house Ravensbury, which stood on the corner of St Mark's Road and Upper Green East. The old pump can be seen in the foreground. At night the fair was lit by naptha flare lamps, 'noisy, smelly and crude'. A great advance on the naptha flares were the high-powered incandescant mantle lamps which burnt paraffin under presssure. 'They gave a splendid light', said Tom Francis. 'When some of the bigger shows generated their own electric light, the flare lamps were doomed.'

147. Showmen's wagons and caravans off Commonside West during a fair on the Green.

148. A gypsy family with their caravan on the Common.

149. A typical party of gypsies on the Common at fair time. At one time gypsies encamped regularly on the Common, usually on that portion between Beddington Lane station and the *Red House* or *Jolly Gardeners*. After control of the Common was vested in the Board of Conservators the gypsies were turned off. Some still lived in caravans on private ground, whilst others eventually moved into houses. When giving his lantern slide lectures in the 1940s Tom Francis used to observe that the old type of gypsy people, with their tanned skin, black hair and white teeth, once so common in Mitcham, were by then seldom seen. A few still made clothes pegs and hawked them from door to door but rarely, it seemed, did they know more than a few words of the old Romany language.

The Wandle and its Industries

Tom Francis prefaced the showing of his slides on the Wandle and its industries with a few observations culled from Hobson's *Book of the Wandle*, which he commended to his listeners. Nearly eleven miles long, and with origins in the springs which once issued strongly from the dip slope of the North Downs, the river had been a trout stream of note, and was still in parts extremely picturesque. Since the first mills were recorded in the Domesday survey of 1086 it had been heavily exploited, both as a source of power, and for the water itself. Numerous industries had come and gone on the stretch of the river which formed the southern boundary of the parish of Mitcham. The first and also one of the last to survive, at least to Tom's early years, was corn milling. Others included the production of leathers, copper working, the grinding of wood for the manufacture of dyes, the bleaching and printing of textiles, paper making, snuff milling and the manufacture of felt and filling materials for use in upholstery. Four watermills partly or wholly within Mitcham were still working in the period covered by Tom Francis's collection: the former Searle's flour mill at the end of Willow Lane had become the Eagle Leather Works of J. S. Deed & Sons in 1884, the Ashby Brothers' lease of the Grove flour mill above Mitcham bridge expired in 1902 and the premises were taken over by the Patent Horse Hair Company, and the nearby Crown Mill of R. R. Whitehead Brothers (destined to be absorbed into the Mitcham Hair and Fibre Mills Ltd.) was producing felt. The fourth, which does not feature in the slide collection, was Rutters' snuff mill at Ravensbury, lying half in Mitcham and half in Morden. The wheel of the fibre mill was still working in 1946, when a sound recording of it in action was broadcast by the B.B.C.

150. Mitcham bridge, carrying the road from Sutton to Mitcham across the Wandle, photographed in 1893 from a footbridge by the disused snuff mill on the southern bank of the river. This was one of the first half-plate photographs taken by Tom Francis. The bridge probably dated to shortly after 1759, when the parishes of Mitcham and Morden were 'presented' to the County magistrates for failing to keep the existing bridge in good repair. The bridge was strengthened and the roadway widened 'some years ago', wrote Tom in the 1940s. The river could also be crossed by a ford (Pl.151), which during the anti-invasion preparations in 1940 was made impassable to road vehicles by iron girders driven into the riverbed, creating what were optimistically regarded as 'tank traps'. These had all been removed by 1945. During Tom Francis's boyhood, fine trout could still be seen in the clear water beneath the bridge, their colouration matching the stony bed of the river. Fishing rights were then the property of a private angling society, known as the 'Wandle Fisheries Association'. The bailiff, Henry Bourne, lived in Wandle Cottage, facing the bridge, and according to Tom used a derelict mill building for raising young trout to restock the river. As a small boy Tom and his friends fished without permission, and without success. 'String and cooked beef had no attraction for trout: we were very incompleat anglers!', he recalled with amusement. Due to the increasingly polluted effluent from industries and the Beddington sewage farm the river gradually lost its purity and, although Captain Harold Bidder, when he was living at Ravensbury Manor in Wandle Road, made an attempt to revive the fishing with young trout, the experiment was not a success, and the fish he introduced soon died. Tom Francis understood the pollution this time to be attributable mainly to drainage from newly tarred road surfaces, and that Croydon Borough Council compensated Bidder for his loss.

151.   Mitcham bridge in about 1900 and, at its side, the ford across the Wandle. The gate on the right gave access to Morden meadow, then private land, but in 1965 it was presented to the National Trust by Merton and Morden Urban District Council and is now incorporated into the Trust's Watermeads property.

152.   Three of the mills upstream from Mitcham bridge can be seen in this early wet-plate photograph taken in 1866. The three-storeyed brick building on the left was the Ashby Brothers' Grove flour mill. The building of the Crown Mill, occupied by the Mitcham flock and felt works, is in the centre of the picture, and to the right of the house facing the camera, which can be dated to about 1851, can be glimpsed the old snuff mill. All three mills depended on the Wandle for power, and the wheel of the felt factory, which later became part of the Mitcham Hair and Fibre Mills, was still in use in the 1940s. Both the flour and felt mills repeatedly suffered damage from fire during the late 19th and early 20th centuries. On the last occasion John Brown, master of the parish's manual pump, irreverently nick-named the 'Old Squirt', made a valiant attempt to overcome the flames by dragging the machine into the river, from where the pumpers worked the levers, standing in water. 'Hot work', observed Tom Francis, 'but their feet were beautifully cool!' When showing this slide, Tom used to recall that fine quality felt was made at the Crown Mill, suitable for piano hammers, padding for harness, felt hats and many other purposes. There was a local tradition that in 1855 the factory had produced felt boots and jerkins for British troops engaged in the Crimean campaign. It has also been claimed that in the early part of the 19th century some of the mill buildings had been used as workshops where wagons used on the Surrey Iron Railway, which ran close by, were repaired. Certainly a number of iron wheels, of the type used on the railway wagons, were utilised at one time to protect the banks of the mill tail from erosion. Over the years several of the wheels have been dislodged by the force of the water, and it has been possible to retrieve them from the river bed.

153. A study dated 1895 of the disused snuff mill on the Morden bank of the river above Mitcham bridge. According to Tom Francis the building seen here collapsed some twenty years before he began compiling his lecture notes.

154. Buildings of Deed's Mill, situated on an artifical island created by a diversion of the river at the southern end of Willow Lane. The great water wheel and main mill buildings are out of view, to the left. Access for vehicles from Willow Lane was by a ford. For a century or more the mill had been used for flour milling, but in 1884 it became the Eagle Leather Works of John S. Deed and Sons, manufacturers of fine white buckskins and other soft leathers. According to Tom Francis, chamois leathers, one of the chief products in the 1940s, could then be seen drying in the adjoining meadows. It was Tom's understanding that Deed's produced the leather from which the scabbard was made for the sword presented by Great Britain to the city of Stalingrad. The quality of the Wandle water was commonly held to be specially suitable for leather dressing, and several other mills, known as 'skinning mills', were to be found upstream. One of these, housed in an old wooden building, was a parchment factory. The *Skinners' Arms*, on the main road to Beddington, was the workers' 'local'.

155.   Harvey and Knight's oilcloth factory in Morden Road, photographed in 1870. The drying sheds extended a considerable distance towards the railway line at the rear. Many old Mitchamers started work here as 'colourboys', and worked on 'until they could work no more'. The floor cloths were printed by hand from carved wooden blocks, each about eighteen inches square. These were produced by local block cutters, and might include strips of brass or brass pins in the case of the more intricate designs. Although production involved such inflammable materials as oil, turpentine and canvas, the wooden factory building escaped disaster by fire and was eventually pulled down. Of the younger generation of Harvey's, Tom and Noel were cricketers of more than local fame, and many other good players also came from amongst the firm's employees. Robert Harvey was a teacher of music and singing, and for some time was organist at the parish church.

156.   The oilcloth manufactured by Harvey and Knight was superseded by cork linoleum, produced by Hayward's, a firm which had a factory on the opposite side of Morden Road. Despite being built of brick, Hayward's linoleum factory met with disaster several times through fires, the aftermath of one of which in the 1890s was photographed by Tom Francis. Bigsby's paint and colour works eventually took over part of the premises, and subsequently this was occupied by Hancock and Corfield, manufacturers of enamelled signs etc. The works was destroyed during an air raid, but the Mitcham rubber works, which was on another part of the former Hayward's site, was still there when Tom Francis was compiling his notes in the mid-1940s.

The Watermeads

The National Trust's Watermeads property on the eastern side of Bishopsford Road comprises some twelve acres of woodland with secluded walks extending mainly along the south bank of the Wandle above Mitcham bridge. The original 11 acres were purchased for £1,050 by the River Wandle Open Spaces Committee, and handed over by them to the Trust in 1913. 'Happy Valley', a further two acres on the opposite side of the road, was presented to the National Trust in 1915 by Richardson Evans in memory of the late Octavia Hill who, with Sir Robert Hunter and Canon H.D. Rawnsley, had been one of the founders of the Trust in 1895. Octavia Hill and her sister Miranda are also to be remembered for their pioneering work in the movement to improve the housing of working people in London, and a stone seat suitably inscribed to Miranda's memory was placed near the 'Jack Pond' in the Watermeads.

Tom Francis had been actively involved in the efforts to preserve the Watermeads, and was for some time chairman of the local committee of the National Trust. He had always been fond of trees, and during the mid 1940s not only planted, and donated, a large number, in the Watermeads and 'Happy Valley', but also encouraged others to do likewise. Few of the varieties selected were indigenous, or suited to a site with a high water table, but the wish at the time was to enhance the visual appearance and interest of the properties with a diversity of form and foliage colour, together with berries which would attract birds.

157. The 'Paper Mill Cut' in the Watermeads. This photograph, which Tom Francis described as having been taken looking towards the river Wandle, shows the artificial 'cut' created to serve a late 18th-century paper mill. This was located a little upstream from Mitcham bridge. All trace of the paper mill has long since disappeared.

158. The 'Mill Cut' in the Watermeads as it appeared *c.*1910, viewed from where a penstock controlled the flow of water into the cut from the Wandle. The red pantiled roofs of the mill cottages near Mitcham bridge can be seen in the distance. What was known as the 'Jack Pond', to the left of the picture, was supplied from the cut itself, but by this time the pond had become much overgrown. It had presented a very different picture during the harsh winters of the 1880s, however, when Bourne the water bailiff festooned the trees with Chinese lanterns, and the pond became a favourite skating place with Mitcham 'society'.

159. This third and final picture in the vicinity of the Watermeads was taken by Tom Francis near the 'Hilly Fields', now part of Poulter Park. He explained that 'the little stream flowed into the Wandle at Deeds Mill'. It was near this picturesque spot that the Gallician gypsies (Pl.47) made their camp.

The Vestry and Local Government

Until the reform of local government structure late in the 19th century, affairs in Mitcham were in the hands of the local vestry, which had responsibilities not only for church matters, but also for many of the functions we now associate with borough and county councils. By Tom Francis's boyhood it had become clear that many of the duties hitherto shouldered by the parish vestries, such as poor relief, burials, education, drainage, and the maintenance of main roads, were better administered by statutory bodies or *ad hoc* boards. The country was divided into urban and rural sanitary authorities in 1872, but a confusing motley of bodies persisted, with a multiplicity of rates. Eventually the situation became simplified following the creation of county councils and county borough councils in 1888, and urban and rural district councils in 1894. Thus Mitcham became a civil parish within the rural district of Croydon in 1895, the first chairman of the parish council being George Parker Bidder Q.C., followed the next year by the vicar, the Rev. D. F. Wilson. Universal franchise had not yet arrived, however, and the right to vote was restricted to ratepayers only.

MITCHAM, 22d *February*, 1798.

AT a Meeting of the INHABITANTS of the parish, convened this day, for the purpose of entering into VOLUNTARY CONTRIBUTIONS for the defence of the country, it was proposed, that books should be opened at the *King's Head Inn*, and at the *Buck's Head Inn*, for receiving any voluntary contributions that might be offered: and it was proposed, that the Landlords of the abovementioned houses should be requested to pay the sums they received into the hands of Mr. HOARE.

IT WAS RESOLVED, That the books should remain open till Monday the 5th of March.

HENRY HOARE, CHAIRMAN.

Previous to the breaking up of the Meeting, the sum of £.301:18:6 was subscribed.

---

160. In 1798, with Napoleon Bonaparte known to be amassing a great invasion force on the French and Belgian coasts, the professional forces in Britain were pitifully small. Typically, it was left to local initiative to plug the gap. On 22 February, at a public meeting in Mitcham chaired by Henry Hoare the London banker (who lived at Mitcham Grove), it had been agreed to launch a special appeal for contributions towards national defence. Such was the support that the incredible sum of £301 18s. 6d. was subscribed before the meeting broke up, and arrangements were made for notices to be prepared inviting further contributions over the course of the next two weeks. In April the vestry formed a committee to 'fix upon a plan to defend this parish from the enemy', and steps were soon being taken to recruit and train an 'Armed Association' comprising one cavalry and one infantry corps. Patriotic fervour was high, and the villagers applied themselves with enthusiasm to drilling and weapon training. Although it was not until 1813 that the Loyal Mitcham Volunteers were finally disbanded, mercifully the threatened invasion never took place, and they were not called to stand against the Imperial Army in defence of their homes and families.

161. Until reform of the poor law administration under the act of 1834, when responsibility for the relief of paupers was gradually transferred to the newly formed boards of guardians, the duty lay with the parish authorities. Whereas since 1737 Mitcham vestry had provided accommodation for the orphaned, destitute, sick and aged in a workhouse, the giving of outdoor relief in the form of a wages supplement, or employment by the parish either directly or under contract with private employers, remained the preferred options in the case of those able to work. This notice, published in 1830 by the vestry, sets out the subsistence level wages available from the parish at a time when, according to Tom Francis, men on farmwork or in the market gardens might receive between 10s. 6d. to 12s. 6d a week. At this time workmen in the local calico printing works could be earning between 10-15s. a week, and a skilled printer as much as 25 shillings. Often faced with increasing costs themselves, employers were tempted to pay as little as possible, and relied on parish relief to save their workforce from starvation. The burden placed upon householders in the form of the poor rate could be heavy (as much as 18s. 0d. in the pound in some parts of Surrey, although not in Mitcham), and in times of depression in the case of a rural parish like Capel, cited by Tom Francis, wages were so low that 40 per cent of the workforce might be receiving relief. Conditions remained harsh for the very poor throughout the rest of the century, and Tom Francis recalled that in his boyhood in the 1870s and '80s the wages of agricultural labourers were still 'terribly low, yet families were reared clean, well-behaved and "respectable" '

MITCHAM.

Vestry Room, Feb. 17, 1830.

At a SPECIAL VESTRY, held this day, pursuant to Notice given in the Church on Sunday last, and which was *numerously* attended, the following SCALE of WAGES for *Paupers* employed by the Parish Officers, was *unanimously* agreed to.

SCALE.

			s.	d.		
A Single Man,	from 16 to 18 Years of Age.		3	6	per Week.	
Ditto,	from 18 to 21	ditto	4	6	ditto.	4 - 6
Ditto,	from 21 and upwards . .		5	0	ditto.	6 - 0
Man and Wife			6	0	ditto.	7 - 6
Ditto,	with 1 Child		7	6	ditto.	9 - 0
Ditto,	with 2 Children		8	0	ditto.	10 - 0
Ditto,	with 3 ditto		9	0	ditto.	11 - 0
Ditto,	with 4 ditto		9	6	ditto.	11 - 6
Ditto,	with 5 and upwards. . . .		10	0	ditto.	12 - 0

The Hours of Work to be from 8 o'Clock in the Morning, until 5 in the Evening.

SIGNED BY ORDER,

JOHN CHART,

Vestry Clerk.

ANNAN. PRINTER. CROYDON.

162.   The old cage, pound and stocks with the *Cricketers* inn, portrayed in a watercolour by John Francis Dixon, a member of the Society of Friends' Mitcham Meeting. The painting, which was produced for use in one of Thomas Francis's calendars, was imaginary, but is a reasonable representation of the Lower Green in about 1830. The cage, or lock-up, dated from 1765 and was demolished in 1887 to make way for the building of the Vestry Hall. It had been intended for the detention of miscreants pending a hearing before the local justices, but was not particularly secure, and escape proved an easy matter. The last man to be detained there made his way to freedom, albeit temporarily, through a hole in the roof!

163.   An interesting old wet-plate photograph of the *Cricketers* and the former village cage, taken *c.*1870. In its final years the building was used to house the parish's manual fire engine, and the walls became popular for bill-posting. In fact, said Tom Francis, 'so many layers of paper and paste had been built up that a local "snob" [cobbler] was said to use it for his boot repairs'. Only the post of the stocks remained standing within Tom's memory, and was deposited, complete with its iron staple, in the basement of the new Vestry Hall. Although an historical curiosity, it was not considered worth keeping, and disappeared many years ago.

First Ratepayer "Well, Sir, wot I says I'll stick to"
2nd Ditto "Wot d'ye mean by that, Sir?"
First Do .. "Wot I say, Sir!"
2nd R . "You're a individual, Sir!"
First R . "You're another, Sir!"
2nd R . "You're a parallelogram, Sir!"
First R .. "You're no gentleman, Sir!"
2nd R .. "You're a humbug, Sir!"

164.   A cartoon by Collingsby of a stormy vestry meeting with the Rev. D. F. Wilson, Edwin Chart, John R. Chart, Thomas Allen (speaking), Robert Richman and William Harwood (back view). 'When any public question rose,/The Vestry met to bicker,/And often even came to blows/Despite the Chairman Vicar./The meeting seldom closed without/Black eyes and nasal bleeding/While ink bottles were flung about/To liven the proceedings.' (R. M. Freeman in 'Truth' quoted by Tom Francis, expressing the hope that in the case of Mitcham this was an exaggeration.)

165.   John Brown, village blacksmith, ironmonger and wheelwright, portrayed by Collingsby. John lived at the shop in The Broadway, Lower Mitcham, identified by Tom Francis as 'where Mrs. Pratt now lives' (in the mid-1940s). 'J.B. was a great politician and critic of the local Parish Officers.' Mitcham's manual fire engine was under his charge, so in a sense John can be seen as a forerunner of the Borough Engineer.

Boy "If you please Mr Tinker, could you mend the manners of Our Vestry?"

166. The parish manual fire engine, taking part in a procession to celebrate the coronation of George V. The driver on this occasion was John Brown junior. Before it was pensioned off the engine was pulled to a fire by a white horse, with boys energetically assisting by 'pushing up' behind. Volunteers might offer their services, or else men be 'pressed' to pump by bribes of free drinks. Once at the fire, with rhythmical chanting of 'beer', the men endeavoured to keep time as they worked at the pump, and to ensure that their reward would not be forgotten. Tom Francis never saw the pump in action, and understood the last time it was used had been when Ashby's flour mill caught fire (and burned down) in 1907. In those days, if help was needed, the Sutton or other neighbouring brigades might be called upon to give assistance. The last incident 'attended' by the manual pump was when a small fire occurred at London House and Tom Francis, having been ordered to 'fetch the brigade', called both the steam powered engine and the 'Old Squirt', just to be on the safe side. In the event the manual was not needed, and modestly remained in the shadow of the trees whilst the men from the 'steamer' doused the flames.

167.   The Vestry Hall was, of course, decorated for Queen Victoria's Diamond Jubilee in 1897. The Hall had been erected 10 years earlier on the site of the old pound, the village lock-up and stocks and was opened on 18 May 1887 by Mrs. Cosmo Bonsor, wife of the member of Parliament for the Wimbledon division. 1887 was the Queen's Golden Jubilee year, and the official opening of the new hall and vestry offices added a local dimension to the celebrations, which concluded with a grand firework display on the Green opposite Mitcham Court. Amongst the names of the parish overseers still to be seen inscribed on the foundation stone is that of Thomas Francis senior. The height of the building to the top of the weather vane is 82 ft., and the clock, high in the tower, was purchased by surviving members of the committee of the 'Original Mitcham Penny Reading' of 1866-73 from surplus funds in their hands. The dials are four feet in diameter, the figures eight inches long, the hour bell weighed about three hundredweight, and the two quarter bells two and a half hundredweight. The volunteer fire brigade's steam engine *Caesar* was housed in the new building where, many years later, the present entrance lobby was constructed. The original public entrance to the parish offices, visible in the photograph, was in the centre. The fire alarm was struck on the big bell of the clock, and could be a very startling summons in the still hours of the night. The bell ceased to strike and the clock was left unlit on the outbreak of war in September 1939. On 1 March 1945 the clock was again illuminated as a trial, and the siren wailed in the night. The clock was officially lit up again on Monday, 23 April 1945. The Vestry Hall, which was destined to become the offices of the new urban district council in 1916, and the town hall when Mitcham attained borough status in 1934, was soon the centre of Mitcham life. Here were held the annual parish meetings in the days of the parish council, and public meetings to hear the candidates for election, often to the delight and amusement of the public. Mitcham in its village days a century ago had, largely, to provide its own entertainment, and here in the Vestry Hall were also held plays and recitals, poetry readings, spelling bees, temperance meetings, learned lectures, Band of Hope concerts, bazaars and socials, smoking concerts, brass band concerts, performances by a local 'nigger' minstrel troupe and visiting performers, badminton matches, political meetings and religious services.

168. Mitcham's steamer fire engine, a second-hand Merryweather No.1 'Volunteer' (seen here in a Coronation procession), was bought by public subscription in 1884. Caesar Czarnikow of Mitcham Court, a wealthy sugar merchant, was a principal contributor to the purchase fund, and appropriately the engine was christened *Caesar*. The brigade were volunteers, with Robert Masters Chart in charge, and Athol Harwood, captain. W. Jenner the ironmonger was engineer, assisted by Alfred Jenner, whilst Freddie Samson, the local vet, acted as driver. The rest of the gallant brigade comprised local lads, including Charlie Hallward ('Spectre' of the *Advertiser*), Tubby Foster, Teddy Powell, Bill Shepherd, Bill Southerton (of the *Cricketers*), Billy Barter the grocer, and Alfred Clarke the doctor's son. Call boy Sam Turner had the duty of arousing the men when the alarm sounded. Great commotion attended the preparations. Horses were collected and harnessed, a fire was started in the boiler to raise steam, and brigade members appeared from all quarters, pulling on their uniforms. On duty the men wore grand brass helmets, but R. M. Chart

and W. Jenner were evidently prepared to risk their bushy beards being singed! Drama heightened with the clatter of the horses' hooves and reached a climax with the sound of the pulsating pump and finally the hissing of water as it was played on the flames. It is hardly surprising that invariably the engine was followed to the scene of the conflagration by scores of hurrying children and adults. Fires at one of Mitcham's many varnish works might be accompanied by 'great flames, smoke and stink', recalled Tom Francis, whilst 'Pain's firework factory supplied explosions, great and small, sometimes fatal', whilst gorse fires on the Common provided the brigade with less dangerous practice. Not all fire incidents were so dramatic, and at times the brigade's response was hardly impressive. Tom Francis remembered one occasion when a child upset a paraffin lamp at London House. The brigade duly answered the summons with their new engine, but before they could raise steam the fire was extinguished by Fred Samson bailing water from the children's bath with his brass helmet. 'Well, I'm glad, Mr. Francis, it has ended like this,' said the crestfallen superintendent turning to Thomas Francis sen., 'but you see we can't get a fire.' A house for the steamer was built in Haydon's yard next to the pond on Lower Green West (near where Preshaw Crescent now stands), but after 1887 *Caesar* was moved to the station designed for it within the new Vestry Hall.

169. A placard at a time when the outskirts of Mitcham had so increased in population that the new residents were able to turn up at a parish meeting, demand better representation on the parish council, and actually succeed in turning many of the old councillors out of office. Later Mitcham was divided into four wards, of four members each. The 'sandwich man' in this photograph was one of the Chippendale family.

170. An electioneering stunt in Mitcham. Fred Harris, dressed in a woman's nightgown, rode through the village in an endeavour to persuade electors to vote for W. Mapp Thompson, an architect by profession, living at Baron Grove. Tom admitted he had forgotten if Fred's effort had the desired effect.

171. A display of posters for candidates at a parish council election in about 1904, pasted on the wall of a building at the rear of the *Cricketers* and the Vestry Hall. The election was well-contested, with 36 candidates standing for 16 seats. Public meetings in the Vestry Hall at election times were entertaining for parishioners, who quite often overcrowded the room.

172. The clock tower at Fair Green replaced the village pump in 1898. It was erected by public subscription to commemorate the Diamond Jubilee of Queen Victoria. Draper Samuel Love of Fair Green was responsible, with Cubison and others, for the collection and exhibited a picture of the proposed cast-iron clock standard in his shop window. He was much upset when Tom Francis told him he preferred the old village pump. The opening ceremony was performed on 29 November 1899 by James Salter-Whiter J.P., chairman of the Croydon Rural District Council. The event was captured for posterity by Tom Francis from a window of Ravensbury, James Drewett's house, which was pulled down to make room for the Majestic Cinema in the 1930s. The clock tower, with its four-faced clock, four gas lamp brackets and drinking fountain, was a source of criticism and expense from the beginning. Owing to the cast-iron casing it was very sensitive to frost, and as a consequence, the clock often stuck. The four faces frequently told different times, and it reached the zenith of its notoriety when it hurriedly started to go backwards! Russell, the jeweller, confided to Tom Francis that the trouble was mainly due to the fact that a four-foot well had to be sunk in the ground for the clock weights. This was often below water level, and the resultant condensation on the works affected the clock's efficient working. Through much of the First World War the clock registered twenty minutes to eleven, and although several attempts were made to induce it to keep good time, improvements never lasted for long. Lloyd George, who for a while lived at Walton-on-the-Hill, actually mentioned the Fair Green clock during a parliamentary debate, comparing it to some of his friends on the Opposition, who could not get a move on! The gas lamps were extinguished for the last time on the outbreak of war on 3 September 1939.

Mitcham en Fête and Village Celebrations

Tom Francis's memories were of a self-contained community, and one in which the energetic had little reason to be bored.

> Mitcham people in those days on the whole did not venture far from home. There was no need to. Wages were small and wants were small, and Mitcham shops could supply them. Recreation had to be obtained locally ... Work absorbed most of people's time, and relaxation was sought in the pubs, in the young men's clubs, in cricket and football, in quoits, gardening, poultry, rabbit, pig and goat keeping, in 'Penny Readings', spelling bees, nigger troupes, choral societies and music.

The old village excelled itself whenever a national or even local event occurred which called for a celebration to mark the occasion. The late 19th and early 20th centuries seem to have provided an unusually rich sequence of opportunities, in the form of royal marriages, jubilees and coronations, and the signing of peace agreements. The jollifications all followed very much the same pattern, with the decoration of houses, shops and public buildings, beflagged streets, pageants, sports, bonfires and fireworks and, of course, processions. All offered attractive subjects for the amateur photographer like Tom Francis and his contemporaries, and a considerable number of the slides in his collection are of the people of late Victorian and Edwardian Mitcham enjoying themselves.

173. The first slide in this selection is a general view of the Cricket Green in 1897 when the village was celebrating the Diamond Jubilee of Queen Victoria. Proceedings had opened with the customary procession in the morning, followed by athletic sports on the Green in the afternoon, and were to close with fireworks and a bonfire in the evening.

174. Sports on the Cricket
Green. In the early days
remembered by Tom Francis
races were arranged in a free
and easy style, and it was only
later, as life became more
sophisticated, that they began
to be held under the rules of the
Amateur Athletics Association.
He recalled that during one of
the jubilee celebrations the
Union Jack in the centre of the
arena flew upside down
throughout the day,
presumably without anyone
worrying unduly.

175. The firemen's race during
the Diamond Jubilee
celebrations. The volunteer fire
brigade had become a village
institution, and was assured of
the support of the whole
community. Firemen's races
and contests, in which the teams
competed in full uniform, drew
large and enthusiastic
audiences.

176.   Here we see the procession of decorated horses and carts rounding the corner of the Cricket Green by the *King's Head* during the celebration of Queen Victoria's Diamond Jubilee.

177.   Although pensioned off, and in reality considered as something of a joke, the 'Old Squirt' seems always to have been included in the village processions. Here, driven by John Brown junior, and pulled by a pony, which if not the original animal, was at least of the same colour, the manual pump is seen trundling sedately along the Causeway in 1911. Sadly, such was the lack of interest in Mitcham's past in later years that the manual pump was allowed to rot in a council yard, and was finally broken for scrap.

178. The coronation of George V in 1911 provided the last opportunity for the village to indulge its love of processions and display before the outbreak of the First World War, after which nothing was to be quite the same. On this occasion there was the usual procession of decorated vehicles, including fire engines, and floats from local factories, fancy costumes, sports on the Green, and illuminations at night. In this slide we see impressively dressed men from two fire crews riding on their bright red steam engines. They are passing the old police station on the Causeway, and are attended as usual by a crowd of admiring small boys.

179. Pageants provided opportunities for dressing up, and fancy dress competitions then, as now, were always popular with the extroverts. In this group photograph, taken in 1911, 'Fot' Chippendale is dressed in smock and neckerchief advocating 'Back to the Land'; Nightingale, dressed as an old time player, recalls Mitcham's great cricketing days when, according to jealous neighbours, the village team never admitted defeat; S. Taylor, for reasons which Tom Francis does not explain in his slide notes, appears as a Dutchman walking on his hands; Frank Reed as 'White Ben' and Albert Francis sports another Dutch costume as 'Zuider Zee', for which he was awarded a prize.

180. Probably the outstanding event in the 1911 Coronation celebrations was the Elizabethan parade, held on the Cricket Green opposite Robert Masters Chart's house, St Mary's. During the 16th century Mitcham had enjoyed considerable popularity as a country resort away from the smells and disease of Tudor London, and many local people donned period costumes for the pageant to recall this 'golden age' in the history of the village. The Bidder family of Ravensbury Manor had a big share in the production, and the undoubted stars of the parade were some of the ladies and gentlemen from the larger houses, who entered into the spirit of the occasion and appeared in costumes which would certainly not have been out of place at the Elizabethan court. In this photograph we see Charles Lack dressed as a 'Beefeater' and Robert Masters Chart, the parish clerk and by profession an architect and surveyor, as Lord Burleigh. The show was voted a great success.

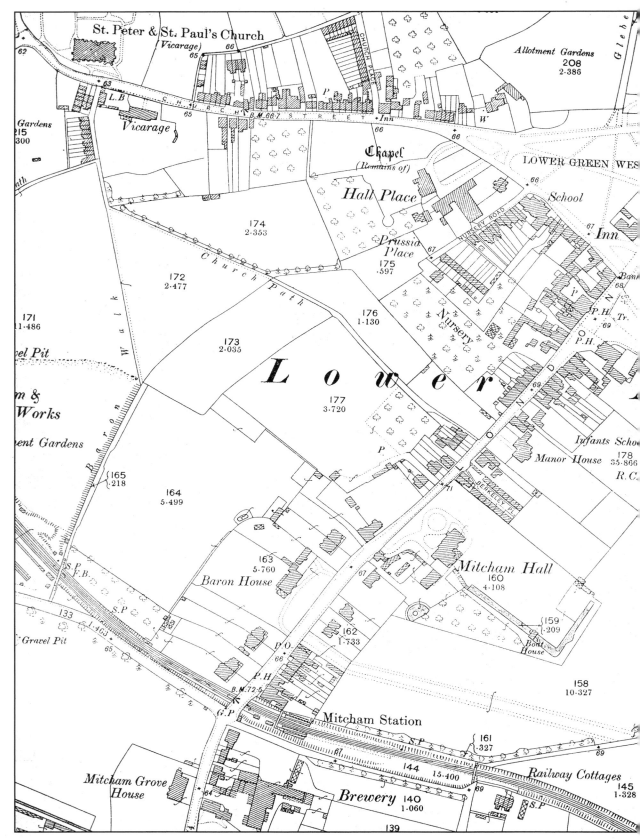

Detail from Second Edition Ordnance Survey Map of 1895.